This Book Belongs To:

....

Christmas 2016

2016

CHRISTMAS

—— WITH ——

Southern Living

2016
CHRISTMAS

— WITH —

Southern Living®

THE COMPLETE GUIDE TO
HOLIDAY COOKING AND DECORATING

SPECIAL BONUS SECTION CELEBRATES THE MAGAZINE'S 50TH YEAR

WITHDRAWN

Welcome

As we celebrate the season this year, we also celebrate 50 years of *Southern Living*. Since 1966, the magazine has endured as *the* resource for Southern food, decorating, and entertaining ideas. It doesn't matter if you live deep in the heart of the South or far from it, *Christmas with Southern Living* delivers holiday inspiration with the turn of every page. Whether your holiday tradition is to host casual family gatherings or formal Christmas feasts, you will find carefully crafted menus and over 100 meticulously tested recipes for every occasion throughout the season. You'll also discover fabulous gifts from the kitchen along with festive packaging ideas—making each gift truly unique. With over 80 pages dedicated to holiday decorating along with resources for getting the look in your own home, we make decking the halls simpler than ever before. Finally, to celebrate our 50th anniversary, we offer a special bonus section highlighting 50 candy and bonbon recipes collected from all five decades of the magazine. So take a seat by the fire, put your feet up, and get in the holiday spirit, *Southern Living*-style.

Merry Christmas!

Katherine Cobbs

Katherine Cobbs
Senior Editor

Contents

Entertain

Forest Feast

Usher in the holiday season with an autumn-meets-winter feast highlighting foraged delights like wild mushrooms, nuts, and woodsy herbs along with company-worthy roast turkey and all the fixin's.

The Menu

SERVES 6 TO 8

FIG-ROSEMARY RYE SMASH

BRUSSELS SPROUT CROSTINI
WITH PUMPKIN BUTTER AND HAZELNUTS

ROASTED BUTTERNUT SQUASH-APPLE SOUP
WITH WALNUT-CHIVE OIL

RUSTIC WILD MUSHROOM-HERB DRESSING

TUSCAN KALE WITH CRISPY GARLIC AND PANCETTA

CRANBERRY-JUNIPER CHUTNEY

HERB-CITRUS SWEET TEA-BRINED TURKEY
WITH CARAMELIZED ONION AND FENNEL GRAVY

BITTERSWEET CHOCOLATE-CHESTNUT TORTE
WITH CHESTNUT BOURBON CREAM

A Warm and Welcoming Entry

Woodsy accents in brown, copper, gray, and green come together in a livable, neutral decorative scheme to carry you through the holiday season and beyond. A long-lasting arrangement of bark, branches, moss, and berries crowned with a gleaming bronze sphere is reflected in a mirror for double the impact. An everlasting wreath need not be evergreen—a mass of nuts, acorns, and dried forest floor finds given a light metallic sheen adds a warm sparkle to the front door and is as welcome an accent at Halloween as it is topped with a conifer bough and bow at Christmas. A baker's wooden dough bowl finds new use as a pretty place to corral packages wrapped and ready for giving. Tiny bark baskets filled with posies made from delicate blossoms make sweet parting favors for family and friends.

Fireside Forest

A verdant centerpiece in many shades
of green with accents of glowing copper serves
as a party focal point for a rustic feast.

Woodland Mantel
Pinecones, bark, candles, and greenery are natural elements that go with any decor.

Fig-Rosemary Rye Smash

MAKES ¾ CUP
**HANDS-ON 10 MINUTES TOTAL 10 MINUTES,
NOT INCLUDING SYRUP**

Sweet-and-savory with a spike of spirit and an herbal syrup infusion, this cocktail is equally delicious with bourbon in place of the rye.

½   cup rye whiskey
¼   cup Fig-Rosemary Honey Syrup
1½   tablespoons fresh lemon juice
2   dashes lemon bitters
Garnishes: reserved fig pieces from Fig-Rosemary Honey
     Syrup, fresh rosemary sprigs, lemon rind strips

Combine first 4 ingredients in a cocktail shaker with ice. Shake vigorously for 30 seconds. Strain into 2 (8-ounce) rocks glasses filled with ice.

NOTE: We tested with Bulleit rye whiskey and Fee Brothers lemon bitters.

Fig-Rosemary Honey Syrup

MAKES ¾ CUP
HANDS-ON 10 MINUTES TOTAL 55 MINUTES

½   cup chopped Mission figs
½   cup honey
1   fresh rosemary sprig
⅔   cup water

Bring all ingredients and ⅔ cup water to a boil over medium-high heat in a small saucepan, stirring constantly. Boil until honey dissolves. Remove from heat, and let stand 15 minutes. Pour through a strainer into a bowl. Reserve figs for garnishing drinks, if desired. Cool syrup completely (about 30 minutes). Store in refrigerator up to 1 week.

Brussels Sprout Crostini with Pumpkin Butter and Hazelnuts

SERVES 6 TO 8
HANDS-ON 20 MINUTES TOTAL 20 MINUTES

This recipe calls for store-bought crostini to help save time, but making your own will always impress your guests.

1   pound Brussels sprouts, thinly shaved
2   tablespoons olive oil
4   garlic cloves, minced
1   teaspoon ground coriander
½   teaspoon kosher salt
¼   teaspoon ancho chili powder
¼   teaspoon ground cumin
1   tablespoon sherry vinegar
2   tablespoons minced fresh chives
1   teaspoon lime or lemon zest
¾   cup homemade or store-bought pumpkin butter
30   homemade or store-bought crostini
½   cup blanched hazelnuts, toasted and coarsely chopped

1. Cook Brussels sprouts in hot oil in a large skillet over medium-high heat, stirring occasionally, until bright green. Cover, reduce heat, and cook 5 minutes or until just tender.

2. Add garlic and next 4 ingredients. Cook, stirring constantly, 1 minute or until fragrant. Add vinegar, stirring to loosen browned bits from bottom of skillet. Remove from heat, and stir in chives and lime zest.

3. Spread about 1 teaspoon pumpkin butter on each crostini. Top with Brussels sprouts mixture and hazelnuts. Serve warm or at room temperature.

NOTE: We tested with McCutcheon's pumpkin butter.

Time-Saver

While a mandoline is ideal for paper-thin slices, it's a bit cumbersome to use with Brussels sprouts. Shave time off prep by shaving the sprouts in a food processor fitted with the slicing disc attachment instead.

Roasted Butternut Squash-Apple Soup

SERVES 6 TO 8
**HANDS-ON 30 MINUTES TOTAL 1 HOUR, 20 MINUTES,
NOT INCLUDING OIL**

The Walnut-Chive Oil can be made 3 days ahead and refrigerated. Remember to bring it to room temperature before serving with the soup. The soup itself can also be made ahead and will be great with lunch the next day.

2½   pounds butternut squash, peeled and cut into
      ¾-inch cubes
2   medium-size Gala apples, peeled and cut into
      ¾-inch cubes
1   medium leek, cut into ½-inch half-moon slices
2   medium shallots, quartered
1   tablespoon finely chopped fresh thyme
1   tablespoon finely chopped fresh sage
2   tablespoons olive oil
1   teaspoon kosher salt
1   teaspoon smoked paprika
½   teaspoon freshly ground black pepper
5   cups chicken broth
1   bay leaf
1   cup heavy cream
Walnut-Chive Oil
Garnish: toasted walnuts

1. Preheat oven to 450°F. Toss together first 10 ingredients in a large bowl; divide between 2 large jelly-roll pans.

2. Bake at 450°F for 30 to 35 minutes or until tender, rotating pans and tossing vegetables halfway through.

3. Transfer vegetables to a large saucepan, and add broth and bay leaf. Bring to a boil, and reduce heat. Simmer 15 minutes or until liquid is reduced slightly.

4. Process mixture, in batches, in a blender until smooth (or use a handheld immersion blender, if desired). Return each batch to pan.

5. Stir in cream and table salt and pepper to taste. Ladle soup into bowls, and drizzle with Walnut-Chive Oil.

Walnut-Chive Oil

MAKES ¼ CUP
HANDS-ON 15 MINUTES TOTAL 35 MINUTES

This bright green oil is a great finishing touch to the Roasted Butternut Squash-Apple Soup.

½   (1-ounce) package fresh chives
⅓   cup olive oil
½   cup coarsely chopped walnuts
¼   teaspoon lemon zest
¼   teaspoon kosher salt

1. Fill a large bowl with ice.

2. Bring 1 cup water to a boil in a small skillet. Add chives, and simmer 5 to 10 seconds or until chives are bright green and tender. Immediately place skillet in ice. Remove chives, and drain on paper towels, squeezing out excess water. Wipe skillet clean.

3. Cook oil and walnuts in skillet over medium-low heat, stirring occasionally, 5 minutes or until walnuts are toasted and fragrant. Pour oil through a strainer into a bowl, reserving toasted walnuts for another use. Let oil cool 20 minutes.

4. Process cooled oil and chives in a blender until smooth. (If desired, pour oil mixture through a cheesecloth-lined wire-mesh strainer into a bowl and discard solids.) Stir in lemon zest and salt.

Fresh Idea

Keep nut oils fresh by storing them in the refrigerator. Their polyunsaturated fats can turn rancid quickly with fluctuations in temperature, so store properly to enjoy them until they're gone.

Rustic Wild Mushroom–Herb Dressing

SERVES 8
HANDS-ON 40 MINUTES TOTAL 3 HOURS, 10 MINUTES

A simple, traditional dressing gets an elegant upgrade with a rosemary–sea salt European-style crusty bread, meaty shiitake and oyster mushrooms, leeks, and dry sherry.

1   (1-pound) day-old rosemary–sea salt–olive oil bread loaf or round, torn or cut into 1-inch pieces (about 10 cups)
2   large leeks
1   cup butter
1½ cups chopped celery
8   ounces shiitake mushrooms, thinly sliced (about 5 cups sliced)
3   (3.5-ounce) packages oyster mushrooms, thinly sliced (about 2 cups sliced)
1½ teaspoons kosher salt
1   teaspoon freshly ground black pepper
⅓   cup dry sherry or dry white wine
⅓   cup chopped fresh flat-leaf parsley
1   tablespoon chopped fresh rosemary
1   tablespoon chopped fresh thyme
1   tablespoon chopped fresh sage
2½ cups chicken broth
2   large eggs, lightly beaten

1. Preheat oven to 250°F. Place bread in a single layer in a jelly-roll pan.

2. Bake at 250°F for 1 hour or until dried out, stirring occasionally. Cool completely (about 20 minutes). Transfer to a large bowl. Increase oven temperature to 350°F.

3. Meanwhile, remove and discard root ends and dark green tops of leeks. Cut in half lengthwise, and rinse thoroughly under cold running water to remove grit and sand. Drain; thinly slice.

4. Melt ½ cup of the butter in a large skillet over medium heat. Add leeks and celery, and cook, stirring occasionally, 12 minutes or until softened and golden brown. Add to bread.

5. Melt remaining ½ cup butter in skillet over medium-high heat. Add all mushrooms, ¾ teaspoon of the kosher salt, and ½ teaspoon of the pepper. Sauté 10 minutes or until golden brown. Stir in sherry; cook 1 minute or until almost completely evaporated.

6. Add mushroom mixture, parsley, next 3 ingredients, and remaining ¾ teaspoon salt and ½ teaspoon pepper to bread mixture. Toss until blended.

7. Whisk together broth and eggs. Pour over bread mixture; toss gently until blended. Let stand 10 minutes, stirring once (for bread to absorb liquid). Spoon into a greased 13- x 9-inch baking dish. Cover with aluminum foil.

8. Bake at 350°F for 40 minutes; uncover and bake 20 minutes or until lightly browned.

Tuscan Kale with Crispy Garlic and Pancetta

SERVES 6
HANDS-ON 25 MINUTES TOTAL 25 MINUTES

Colors of red and green will make you think "Christmas" as soon as this dish hits the table.

4   ounces thinly sliced pancetta, cut into thin strips
2   tablespoons olive oil
6   garlic cloves, thinly sliced
4   (½-pound) bunches Tuscan (lacinato) kale, stemmed and cut into bite-size pieces
2   tablespoons apple cider vinegar
1   teaspoon lemon zest

1. Cook pancetta in hot oil in a Dutch oven over medium-low heat 8 minutes or until pancetta is crisp. Transfer pancetta to a paper towel-lined plate, using a slotted spoon, reserving drippings in Dutch oven.

2. Increase heat to medium, and add garlic to hot drippings; cook 3 minutes or until browned (do not burn). Transfer to a second paper towel-lined plate, using a slotted spoon.

3. Increase heat to medium-high, and add kale to Dutch oven. Cook, tossing with tongs, until coated with oil. Cover and cook, tossing occasionally, 3 minutes or until wilted and tender. Add vinegar, and remove from heat. Stir in lemon zest, and season with kosher salt and freshly ground pepper to taste. Top with crispy pancetta and garlic, and serve immediately.

Cranberry-Juniper Chutney

MAKES **ABOUT 4 CUPS**
HANDS-ON **10 MINUTES** TOTAL **3 HOURS, 40 MINUTES**

Tart, woodsy, yet bright, this chutney is the poster child for ease and elegance. Make up to 1 week ahead and bring to room temperature before serving with Herb-Citrus Sweet Tea-Brined Turkey with Caramelized Onion and Fennel Gravy.

2 (12-ounce) bags fresh or frozen cranberries (about 5 cups)
¾ cup firmly packed dark brown sugar
¼ cup fresh orange juice
6 juniper berries, crushed
1 garlic clove, minced
¼ teaspoon kosher salt

1. Combine all ingredients in a 3½- to 5-quart slow cooker. Cover and cook on LOW 3½ to 4 hours or until cranberries have burst and sauce has thickened slightly.

2. Cool completely (about 1 hour). Store in an airtight container in refrigerator up to 1 week. Serve chilled or at room temperature.

NOTE: If you use frozen cranberries, rinse and drain them before placing in the slow cooker.

Herb-Citrus Sweet Tea-Brined Turkey with Caramelized Onion and Fennel Gravy

SERVES 6 TO 8
HANDS-ON 1 HOUR, 40 MINUTES TOTAL 7 HOURS,
20 MINUTES, PLUS 24 HOURS FOR BRINING

Gone are the days of dry, flavorless turkey breasts and rubbery skin. With the succulently tender meat and unbelievably crispy skin, you won't want to make turkey any other way again. If your turkey is frozen, begin thawing in the refrigerator 2 to 3 days in advance.

TURKEY:

- ¾ cup kosher salt
- 1 gallon brewed sweet tea
- ¼ cup black peppercorns
- 3 tablespoons fennel seeds, crushed
- 3 tablespoons coriander seeds, crushed
- 10 garlic cloves, smashed
- 3 bay leaves
- 1 (12- to 14-pound) whole turkey
- 1 large fennel bulb, trimmed and cut into 1-inch wedges
- 1 large Vidalia onion, cut into 1-inch wedges
- 3 fresh thyme sprigs
- 2 fresh oregano sprigs
- Kitchen string

HERB-CITRUS BUTTER:

- 1 cup unsalted butter, softened
- 2 tablespoons finely chopped fresh oregano
- 2½ teaspoons lemon zest
- 2½ teaspoons orange zest
- 2 teaspoons ground coriander
- ½ teaspoon freshly ground black pepper
- 1 tablespoon Dijon mustard

CARAMELIZED ONION AND FENNEL GRAVY:

- 1 medium parsnip, cut into 1-inch pieces
- 3 celery ribs with leaves, cut into 1-inch pieces
- ½ cup gin
- 1 (32-ounce) container chicken broth

1. Prepare Turkey: Bring first 7 ingredients and 1 gallon water to a boil in a large stock pot. Let cool to room temperature (about 1 hour). Remove giblets and neck from turkey. Place turkey and brine in a very large food-safe container, and weight with plates, if necessary, to keep turkey submerged. Chill 24 hours.

2. Preheat oven to 325°F. Remove turkey from brine, and pat dry. Let stand at room temperature 1 hour.

3. Meanwhile, prepare Herb-Citrus Butter: Stir together butter and next 5 ingredients. Melt half of butter mixture in a small saucepan over low heat.

4. Stir mustard into remaining half of butter mixture, and spread underneath skin of turkey thighs, breasts, and legs.

5. Place fennel, onion, thyme, oregano, and ½ cup water in a single layer in a large roasting pan. Place turkey, breast side up, on a lightly greased roasting rack, and place on top of vegetables in pan. Tie ends of turkey legs together with string; tuck wingtips under.

6. Bake at 325°F for 3 hours and 15 minutes to 4 hours or until a meat thermometer inserted into thickest portion of thigh registers 165°F, basting every 30 minutes with pan juices and melted herb butter. Shield with aluminum foil after 1½ hours to prevent excessive browning, if necessary.

7. Remove turkey from oven, and let stand 30 minutes. Transfer turkey to a serving platter. Pour pan drippings through a wire-mesh strainer into a bowl. Discard all solids except fennel and onion. (Do not wipe pan clean.)

8. Prepare Caramelized Onion and Fennel Gravy: Place parsnip and celery in roasting pan. Cook over medium heat 8 minutes or until a deep golden brown. Add fennel and onion; cook 2 minutes or until beginning to brown. Remove from heat, and stir in gin, scraping bottom of pan to loosen browned bits.

9. Return to heat, and cook 1 minute or until liquid has almost evaporated. Add broth, and bring to a boil. Reduce heat, and simmer 10 minutes or until slightly thickened.

10. Process gravy in a blender or food processor until pureed. Return to skillet, and stir in reserved pan drippings. Season with salt and pepper to taste, and serve with turkey.

Bittersweet Chocolate-Chestnut Torte

SERVES 8
HANDS-ON 20 MINUTES TOTAL 2 HOURS, 40 MINUTES, INCLUDING CREAM

Look for high-quality French sweetened chestnut puree at specialty markets and online. You'll need 1 (17.6-ounce) can to prepare the torte and the accompanying cream.

Parchment paper
4   tablespoons unsweetened cocoa
6   ounces bittersweet chocolate baking bar, chopped
½   cup unsalted butter, softened
½   cup sugar
5   large eggs, separated
1   cup sweetened chestnut puree
¼   cup all-purpose flour
¼   teaspoon table salt
Chestnut Bourbon Cream
Chocolate shavings

1. Preheat oven to 350°F. Grease a 9-inch springform pan; line bottom with parchment paper, and grease parchment. Dust lightly with 1 tablespoon of the cocoa.

2. Microwave bittersweet chocolate in a small microwave-safe bowl at HIGH 1 minute or until melted, stirring after 30 seconds. Let cool 5 minutes.

3. Beat butter and ¼ cup of the sugar at medium speed with an electric mixer until light and fluffy. Add egg yolks, one at a time, beating until blended. Gradually beat in chestnut puree and melted chocolate until well blended. Combine flour, remaining 3 tablespoons cocoa, and salt; gradually add to butter mixture, beating just until blended.

4. Beat egg whites at high speed with an electric mixer until foamy. Gradually add remaining ¼ cup sugar, 1 tablespoon at a time, beating until stiff peaks form. Fold one-fourth of egg whites into chocolate mixture; gently fold in remaining egg whites. Pour into prepared pan, and smooth top of batter.

5. Bake at 350°F for 40 to 45 minutes or until a wooden pick inserted in center comes out with a few moist crumbs. Cool completely in pan on a wire rack (about 1½ hours). Run a sharp knife or offset spatula around sides of pan. Remove sides of pan. Transfer torte to a serving platter; top with Chestnut Bourbon Cream and chocolate shavings.

NOTE: We tested with Ghirardelli Bittersweet Chocolate Baking Bar.

Chestnut Bourbon Cream

MAKES ABOUT 2½ CUPS
HANDS-ON 5 MINUTES TOTAL 5 MINUTES

1   cup heavy cream
⅓   cup sweetened chestnut puree
1   tablespoon bourbon

Beat together all ingredients at medium speed with an electric mixer until well blended; beat at high speed until soft peaks form.

NOTE: We tested with Roland Chestnut Cream for sweetened chestnut puree.

Fresh Idea

For a true taste of the South, seek out chocolate for your recipes from one of the Southern chocolatiers popping up around the region, such as French Broad in North Carolina, Olive & Sinclair in Tennessee, or Paul Thomas Chocolates in Georgia.

Hanging of the Green Brunch

Symbols of eternity and everlasting promise because of their changeless nature, evergreens are an enduring part of the Christmas tradition. Mark the beginning of the season decorating with family and friends then sharing a midmorning meal.

The Menu

SERVES 4 TO 6

SPICY BLOODY MARYS

GINGER MANGOMOSAS

WINTER CITRUS SALAD

LEMON-ROSEMARY DROP BISCUITS

SALTED BROWN SUGAR BUTTER

SMOKED GRITS

SAUSAGE AND ROASTED TOMATO RAGOÛT

BAKED EGGS IN GARLIC-CREAMED KALE

SWEET SRIRACHA BACON

CINNAMON-APPLE-BOURBON BREAD PUDDING

The Holly and the Ivy

Gather natural materials from the yard to mix
with flower shop finds and deck the house inside
and out. Look beyond pine, fir, and holly for
evergreen materials that will add uncommon interest
to an array of arrangements. A porch bed swing
gets dressed for the holidays with pillows,
a cozy throw, and garlands of conifer boughs,
boxwood, and ribbon. Winterberry and cypress
add color and texture to the lamppost, while seeded
eucalyptus and brunia fill out wreaths on
the garden gate. Pinecones, fruit, seeds, and berries
make lovely accents for holiday packages.

Holiday Cheer

A spray of Christmas-red tulips and cluster of amaryllis beckon guests to the bar.

Spicy Bloody Marys

SERVES 4 TO 6
HANDS-ON 10 MINUTES TOTAL 10 MINUTES

Bloody Marys are a classic brunch favorite. Make these easy by setting up your bar with homemade Bloody Mary mix and premium vodka so guests can mix their own. We suggest using Zing Zang Bloody Mary mix for the best results.

Stir together 1 (32-ounce) bottle Bloody Mary mix, juice and zest of 1 lime, 2 tablespoons prepared horseradish, 1 tablespoon Worcestershire sauce, and ¼ teaspoon celery salt in a large pitcher. Serve over ice with a shot of premium vodka in tall glasses with an assortment of garnishes (such as pickled green beans, celery sticks, olives, and whole pickled okra).

Ginger Mangomosas

SERVES 6
HANDS-ON 5 MINUTES TOTAL 5 MINUTES

Try this twist on the traditional mimosa featuring spicy ginger and sweet, rich mango flavors cut with your favorite bottle of bubbly. If you want a sweeter drink, use Moscato instead of Champagne.

Stir together 4 cups orange-mango juice and 4 tablespoons ginger juice in a large pitcher. Place small pieces of crystallized ginger in 6 Champagne flutes, and fill each with equal amounts of sparkling wine (or Champagne) and juice mixture.

NOTE: We tested with Naked brand orange-mango juice and Ginger People ginger juice.

Silver Bells

Potted trees, moss, pomegranates, pears, and garden clippings create a holiday wonderland. Candles and silvery accents add elegant sparkle to a room ready for a season of entertaining.

Winter Citrus Salad

SERVES 6
HANDS-ON 20 MINUTES TOTAL 20 MINUTES

The fresh, bright flavors of winter citrus temper fennel's sweetness and marry beautifully with the peppery bite of arugula and radishes. You can make the vinaigrette and slice the radishes, fennel, and grapefruit up to 1 day ahead. Keep chilled.

8	medium radishes, trimmed
1	medium-size fennel bulb, halved and cored
2	Ruby Red grapefruit
2	tablespoons minced shallots
1	tablespoon chopped fennel fronds
2	tablespoons sherry vinegar
1	tablespoon Dijon mustard
1	teaspoon honey
½	teaspoon kosher salt
⅛	teaspoon freshly ground black pepper
½	cup olive oil
1	(5-ounce) package baby arugula

1. Cut radishes and fennel into very thin slices (about ⅛-inch thick), using a mandoline. Place in a medium bowl.

2. Grate zest from 1 grapefruit to equal 1 teaspoon. Cut peel and pith from both grapefruits; cut crosswise into ¼-inch slices.

3. Whisk together grapefruit zest, shallots, and next 6 ingredients in a small bowl. Gradually add oil, whisking constantly until blended.

4. Toss arugula with 3 tablespoons dressing; place on a large serving platter. Toss fennel mixture with 2 tablespoons dressing; place on top of arugula. Arrange grapefruit slices around arugula; drizzle with additional dressing. Serve immediately.

Holiday Helper

A mandoline makes the paper-thin slices of radishes and fennel here, but it is also a great tool to use with an array of vegetables for holiday canapés and garnishes. It makes prep fast, easy, and the finished results chef-quality.

Lemon-Rosemary Drop Biscuits

MAKES 14 BISCUITS
HANDS-ON 10 MINUTES TOTAL 25 MINUTES

Bright lemon and rosemary complement the richness of these classic drop biscuits and pair well with a number of toppings, such as sweet, creamy butter or raspberry preserves. Give them as a gift with little crocks of the savory-sweet Salted Brown Sugar Butter.

3½	cups self-rising soft-wheat flour
2¼	teaspoons baking powder
3	tablespoons sugar
1	tablespoon finely chopped fresh rosemary
½	cup cold butter, cut into pieces
1	cup cold buttermilk
½	cup cold heavy cream
1	teaspoon lemon zest
	Parchment paper
1	tablespoon butter, melted

1. Preheat oven to 500°F. Whisk together flour, baking powder, 2 tablespoons of the sugar, and rosemary in a large bowl. Cut in cold butter with a pastry blender or fork until mixture forms a coarse meal.

2. Whisk together buttermilk, cream, and lemon zest; add to flour mixture, and stir with a fork just until dry ingredients are moistened.

3. Drop dough by ¼ cupfuls 2 inches apart onto parchment paper-lined baking sheets; brush with melted butter, and sprinkle with remaining 1 tablespoon sugar.

4. Bake at 500°F for 12 to 15 minutes or until golden brown.

NOTE: We tested with White Lily self-rising wheat flour.

Salted Brown Sugar Butter

MAKES 1 (6-INCH) LOG
HANDS-ON 5 MINUTES TOTAL 2 HOURS, 5 MINUTES

You will find endless dishes in which to use this butter, from topping cooked carrots and roasted root vegetables to slathering on dinner rolls and muffins.

1   cup unsalted butter, softened
¼   cup firmly packed brown sugar
1   tablespoon flaky sea salt

1. Beat butter and brown sugar at medium speed with an electric mixer 3 minutes or until light and creamy; fold in sea salt.

2. Place mixture on a large piece of plastic wrap. Bring 1 side of plastic wrap over mixture. Hold down other end of plastic wrap. Place flat edge of a baking sheet or other sturdy, flat object next to butter on plastic wrap. Using your other hand, hold end of baking sheet, and push bottom of baking sheet away from you into base of butter mixture, forming a 6- x 2-inch log. Chill 2 hours or until firm.

Smoked Grits

SERVES 6
HANDS-ON 20 MINUTES TOTAL 1 HOUR, 10 MINUTES

Smoky-flavored, creamy grits are a fantastic way to delight your guests at brunch. The smoking process is much easier than you might think. Simply use your stove to impart rich flavor into plain grits, making them a seemingly luxurious ingredient.

1   cup hickory wood chips
1   cup uncooked stone-ground grits
2   cups milk
1½ teaspoons kosher salt
1   cup (4 ounces) shredded Parmesan cheese
¼   cup butter

1. Pierce 10 holes in bottom of a 13- x 9-inch disposable aluminum pan. Arrange wood chips over holes. Place grits on opposite side of pan.

2. Place pan on stovetop burner with holes over burner; heat burner to medium-high until wood chips begin to smoke. Reduce heat to medium; cover pan with aluminum foil, and seal tightly. Cook 2 minutes. Remove from heat, and uncover; set foil aside.

3. Remove wood chips, using tongs, and place on foil to cool. Transfer smoked grits to a bowl. (Be careful to not include any wood fragments.)

4. Bring 3½ cups water, milk, and salt to a boil in a medium saucepan over medium-high heat. Gradually whisk in grits. Reduce heat, and simmer, stirring often, 50 minutes or until thickened and tender. Stir in cheese and butter until melted. Serve immediately.

NOTE: You can also use regular (not stone-ground) grits for this recipe; just reduce the water to 2 cups. We tested with McEwen & Sons stone ground grits.

Time-Saver

You can make the Sausage and Roasted Tomato Ragoût 1 to 2 days ahead through Step 3.

Sausage and Roasted Tomato Ragoût

SERVES 6
HANDS-ON 30 MINUTES TOTAL 55 MINUTES

Roasting tomatoes and shallots brings out their natural sweetness and amplifies the savory aspects of them as well. To save yourself some valuable time, make this mixture a day or two ahead of time, and store in a container in the refrigerator, as the flavors will deepen over a few days.

2   pints cherry tomatoes
6   shallots, cut into ¼-inch slices (about 2 cups)
2   large fresh thyme sprigs
¼   cup olive oil
1   pound smoked hickory sausage, cut into ¼-inch slices
1   cup diced sweet onion
1   tablespoon chopped fresh thyme
2   tablespoons all-purpose flour
1½ cups chicken broth
¼   cup chopped fresh flat-leaf parsley

1. Preheat oven to 400°F. Place first 4 ingredients in a medium bowl; season generously with salt and pepper to taste, and toss to coat. Pour onto a jelly-roll pan, and spread in an even layer.

2. Bake at 400°F for 25 to 30 minutes or until tomatoes are very tender and most of liquid has thickened. Remove from oven, and cool slightly.

3. Discard thyme sprigs, and transfer tomato mixture to a medium bowl, scraping oil and browned bits from pan into bowl.

4. Cook sausage in a large skillet over medium-high heat 6 minutes or until browned. Transfer to a paper towel-lined plate, reserving 2 tablespoons drippings in skillet.

5. Add onion and chopped thyme to hot drippings, and sauté 4 to 5 minutes. Sprinkle with flour, and cook, stirring constantly, 1 minute. Add broth, stirring to loosen browned bits from bottom of skillet. Cook until mixture thickens. Stir in sausage, tomato mixture, and any accumulated juices from tomatoes. Reduce heat to low, and simmer 5 minutes. Season with table salt and pepper to taste. Stir in parsley.

NOTE: We tested with Conecuh Original Smoked Sausage.

Baked Eggs in Garlic-Creamed Kale

SERVES 6
HANDS-ON 40 MINUTES TOTAL 55 MINUTES

Individual portions of baked eggs in a ramekin of creamy roasted garlic and baby kale are easy to make ahead and pop in the oven the morning of your brunch.

1	cup heavy cream
6	garlic cloves, peeled and crushed
Dash of freshly ground nutmeg	
¼	teaspoon table salt
¼	teaspoon freshly ground black pepper
2	tablespoons olive oil
1	(11-ounce) container baby kale
½	cup grated Parmesan cheese
6	large eggs
1	cup panko (Japanese breadcrumbs)
2	tablespoons chopped fresh parsley
1	teaspoon lemon zest

1. Preheat oven to 400°F. Combine cream and garlic in a medium saucepan over medium heat. Bring to a low simmer, reduce heat, and cook 15 minutes or until garlic is very tender. Whisk in nutmeg, salt, and pepper. Remove from heat.

2. Heat 1 tablespoon of the oil in a large skillet over medium-high heat. Gradually add kale, stirring between batches, until kale is wilted. Cook 4 minutes or until most of liquid has evaporated. Gently mash any whole garlic cloves into cream mixture. Stir cream mixture into kale. Cook over medium heat 5 minutes or until thickened. Stir in ¼ cup of the Parmesan cheese. Remove from heat.

3. Coat 6 (10-ounce) ramekins with cooking spray. Place on a jelly-roll pan. Spoon ⅓ cup kale mixture into each ramekin. Crack 1 egg into each ramekin, and sprinkle with desired amount of salt and pepper.

4. Bake at 400°F for 15 to 17 minutes or until whites are set and yolks are still runny, rotating pan halfway through baking (or as needed for even cooking).

5. Meanwhile, combine panko, parsley, lemon zest, and remaining 1 tablespoon oil and ¼ cup Parmesan cheese in a small bowl.

6. Cook panko mixture in a small skillet over medium-high heat, stirring often, 3 to 5 minutes or until panko is golden and very crispy.

7. Remove ramekins from oven, and top with toasted panko mixture before serving.

Sweet Sriracha Bacon

SERVES 6
HANDS-ON 15 MINUTES TOTAL 55 MINUTES

Sweet brown sugar and spicy Sriracha cloak crispy bacon slices to make your brunch guests crazy with delight. Do yourself a favor and double this recipe— you will need it! If, however, there are any leftovers, crumble them on a salad or mix into cornbread batter before baking.

12	thick-cut hickory-smoked bacon slices
½	cup firmly packed brown sugar
3	tablespoons Asian hot chili sauce (such as Sriracha)

Parchment paper

1. Preheat oven to 375°F. Arrange bacon in a single layer on a lightly greased wire rack in an aluminum foil-lined broiler pan. Bake 10 minutes or just until edges begin to curl.

2. Meanwhile, stir together brown sugar and hot chili sauce in a small bowl until sugar dissolves.

3. Remove bacon from oven, and place in a medium bowl. Add 2 tablespoons sugar mixture, tossing to coat. Return bacon to wire rack, and brush tops of slices with sugar mixture.

4. Bake at 375°F for 20 minutes. Brush with sugar mixture, and bake 10 to 15 minutes or until bacon is crisp and browned, rotating pan if needed for even browning.

5. Cool on wire rack 1 to 2 minutes. Transfer bacon to a parchment paper-lined plate or pan, and cool 5 minutes (bacon will crisp as it cools).

Time-Saver

You can prepare the Baked Eggs in Garlic-Creamed Kale as directed in Steps 1 and 2. Refrigerate creamed kale mixture up to 3 days. Prepare the panko mixture as directed in Steps 5 and 6, and store in an airtight container at room temperature up to 1 day ahead. Crisp panko mixture in a skillet before using.

Cinnamon-Apple-Bourbon Bread Pudding

SERVES 6
HANDS-ON 15 MINUTES TOTAL 1 HOUR, 20 MINUTES

This ooey-gooey decadent dessert is a snap to put together and will delight children and adults alike. Using frozen cinnamon rolls makes your job much easier, and your dessert will still be delightfully homemade in appearance and flavor. If you have leftover cinnamon rolls from a day or two ago, use those and save the extra step of baking frozen rolls for the recipe. The bourbon adds a bit of special flavor but can be omitted.

1   (16-ounce) package frozen cinnamon rolls, thawed
Parchment paper
2   tablespoons butter
1   large Fuji apple, peeled and diced (about 1½ cups)
¼   cup firmly packed brown sugar
½   teaspoon ground cinnamon
¼   teaspoon table salt
3   tablespoons bourbon
2   large eggs
¾   cup half-and-half
1   teaspoon vanilla extract
¾   cup chopped pecans
Garnishes: whipped cream, ground cinnamon

1. Preheat oven to 375°F. Break cinnamon rolls apart, and place 1 to 2 inches apart on a parchment paper-lined baking sheet; reserve icing packet.

2. Bake at 375°F for 12 to 15 minutes or until browned. Cool 10 minutes; tear into 1½-inch pieces.

3. Melt 1 tablespoon of the butter in a large skillet over medium-high heat. Add apple, and sauté 3 minutes or just until beginning to brown. Add 2 tablespoons of the brown sugar, cinnamon, and salt; cook 1 minute, stirring constantly. Remove from heat, and stir in bourbon. Cool 10 minutes.

4. Whisk together eggs, half-and-half, and vanilla in a large bowl; stir in apple mixture and cinnamon roll pieces. Spoon mixture into a lightly greased 8-inch square (2-quart) baking dish.

5. Microwave remaining 1 tablespoon butter in a small microwave-safe bowl at HIGH 30 seconds or until melted; stir in pecans and remaining 2 tablespoons brown sugar. Sprinkle over mixture in baking dish. Place baking dish in a 13- x 9-inch pan; fill pan with hot water to reach halfway up sides of baking dish.

6. Bake at 375°F for 35 minutes or until golden brown and set (a knife inserted in center should come out clean). Drizzle reserved icing over bread pudding.

NOTE: We tested with Sister Schubert's Bake & Serve Cinnamon Rolls.

Fresh Idea

If time permits, gild the decadent-dessert lily by making an old-fashioned, spiked custard sauce to drizzle on top in place of a dollop of whipped cream for an over-the-top sweet ending.

CUSTARD-WHISKEY SAUCE: Bring 1 cup sugar, ½ cup butter, and ½ cup half-and-half to a boil in a saucepan over medium heat, stirring until sugar dissolves. Reduce heat and simmer 5 minutes. Cool; stir in 2 tablespoons bourbon or ½ teaspoon vanilla extract. Makes 1½ cups.

Bake-and-Take Cookie Party

Holiday baking is a beloved tradition around the globe. Share the making-and-baking fun with friends by hosting a memorable cookie bash that yields fresh-baked goodies for nibbling and taking home.

The Menu

SERVES 8 TO 10

CRANBERRY-OATMEAL COOKIE BARK

PECAN LINZER COOKIES

SANTA'S FAVORITE COOKIES

CREAM CHEESE-PEPPER JELLY
THUMBPRINTS

PEPPERMINT CANDY CANE TWISTS

GINGERBREAD HOUSE CUTOUTS

CHAI-SPICED SPRITZ COOKIES

DARK CHOCOLATE CRINKLES

AMBROSIA MACAROONS

"O Christmas Tree"

Bedecked and bedazzled with miniature tools—
measuring spoons, tiny copper pans, vintage cookie
cutters, and garland—a potted tabletop tree is
the perfect centerpiece for the Christmas kitchen
that's sure to make cooks of all ages smile.

All I Want for Christmas

Who doesn't want fresh-baked, made-from-scratch cookies? Share in the work and you and your guests will reap the rewards: multiple batches of cookies to divide, to enjoy, or to give to others. Make the party as festive a holiday occasion as it is a time-saving one. An assortment of cookie cutters can do double-duty as decorative elements on the tree and as tools for guest bakers to use to bake up their sweetest creations. A wreath of brass jingle bells adds a safe shimmer above the stovetop, while the counter beside has snacks and baking supplies at the ready.

Cranberry-Oatmeal Cookie Bark

MAKES 2 DOZEN
HANDS-ON 10 MINUTES TOTAL 1 HOUR, 30 MINUTES

This stir-together cookie dough couldn't be easier. No need to portion the dough or bake several batches. For an adult cookie swap, sprinkle the cookie bark with chopped pistachios or walnuts after drizzling with chocolate. Baking on the lower end of the bake time will produce a chewier bark, while baking longer will produce bark that is crispy throughout.

¾ cup butter, melted
½ cup firmly packed brown sugar
½ cup granulated sugar
1 teaspoon orange zest
1 teaspoon vanilla extract
1¼ cups all-purpose flour
½ teaspoon baking soda
¼ teaspoon table salt
¾ cup uncooked quick-cooking oats
¾ cup sweetened dried cranberries
Parchment paper
½ (4-ounce) bittersweet chocolate baking bar, chopped

1. Preheat oven to 350°F. Stir together first 5 ingredients in a large bowl until well blended. Combine flour, baking soda, and salt; stir into butter mixture. Stir in oats and cranberries (dough will be slightly crumbly).

2. Press dough into a 12- x 10-inch rectangle (about ¼-inch thick) on a parchment paper-lined baking sheet.

3. Bake at 350°F for 25 to 30 minutes or until golden brown and firm. Cool on baking sheet on a wire rack 10 minutes; slide cookie, with parchment paper, onto a wire rack, and cool completely (about 30 minutes). Break into pieces.

4. Arrange cookie pieces on a baking sheet lined with new parchment paper. Microwave chocolate in a small microwave-safe bowl 1 minute or until melted, stirring after 30 seconds. Drizzle chocolate over cookie pieces; chill 15 minutes or until chocolate is set.

Pecan Linzer Cookies

MAKES 2 DOZEN
HANDS-ON 25 MINUTES TOTAL 3 HOURS

This Southern twist on a traditional cookie is a festive addition to a cookie party. Use any flavor jam or jelly you prefer.

2½ cups all-purpose flour
¾ cup pecan halves
½ teaspoon baking powder
½ teaspoon table salt
¼ teaspoon ground cinnamon
1 cup butter, softened
½ cup granulated sugar
1 large egg
1 teaspoon vanilla extract
Parchment paper
1 tablespoon powdered sugar
½ cup cherry jam

1. Pulse first 5 ingredients in a food processor until pecans are finely ground.

2. Beat butter and granulated sugar at medium speed with an electric mixer 3 minutes or until light and fluffy. Beat in egg and vanilla. Gradually add flour mixture, beating on low speed just until combined.

3. Divide dough in half; shape into 2 (¾-inch-thick) disks. Wrap each disk in plastic wrap, and chill 2 hours.

4. Preheat oven to 350°F. Roll each disk to ⅛-inch thickness on a floured surface. Cut each disk into 24 (2½-inch) fluted rounds, rerolling scraps as needed. Place dough rounds 1 inch apart on parchment paper-lined baking sheets. Cut centers out of half of cookies using 1½-inch shaped cutters.

5. Bake at 350°F for 12 to 14 minutes or until edges are golden. (If desired, place cut centers of dough on a separate parchment paper-lined baking sheet, and bake 9 to 11 minutes.) Cool on baking sheet on a wire rack 5 minutes; transfer to rack, and cool completely (about 20 minutes).

6. Sprinkle powdered sugar over hollow cookies. Pulse jam in a food processor until pureed. Spread about 1 teaspoon jam onto each solid cookie; top with cut-out cookies.

Santa's Favorite Cookies

MAKES 4 DOZEN
HANDS-ON 15 MINUTES TOTAL 1 HOUR, 5 MINUTES

This is a "kitchen sink" cookie of sorts. Swap out the mix-ins for your kids' favorites. The combination of cake flour and bread flour may seem odd, but it produces a cookie with the perfect tenderness and chew. This is the ideal make-ahead dough; it keeps very well in the refrigerator for up to 2 weeks. Have some on hand throughout the holiday season to bake fresh cookies at the spur of the moment for gifts, guests, or parties.

- 2 cups plus 2 tablespoons cake flour
- 1¾ cups bread flour
- 1½ teaspoons baking powder
- 1¼ teaspoons baking soda
- 1 teaspoon table salt
- 1¼ cups unsalted butter, softened
- 1¼ cups firmly packed light brown sugar
- 1 cup granulated sugar
- 2 large eggs
- 2 teaspoons vanilla extract
- 1¼ cups chopped toasted pecans
- 1 cup red and green candy-coated milk chocolate pieces
- ¾ cup sweetened flaked coconut
- 2 (4-ounce) bittersweet chocolate baking bars, chopped
- Parchment paper

1. Preheat oven to 375°F. Whisk together first 5 ingredients in a medium bowl. Beat together butter and both sugars at medium speed with a heavy-duty electric stand mixer 3 to 5 minutes or until very light and fluffy. Beat in eggs, one at a time, until blended. Beat in vanilla. Gradually add flour mixture, beating at low speed until blended. Stir in pecans and next 3 ingredients.

2. Place heaping scoopfuls of dough about 2 inches apart on large parchment paper-lined baking sheets, using a 1-ounce cookie scoop.

3. Bake at 375°F for 13 to 15 minutes or until golden brown but with centers still soft. Cool on baking sheet on a wire rack 5 minutes; transfer to wire rack, and cool completely (about 20 minutes).

NOTE: If you don't have a cookie scoop, roll the dough into 1½-inch balls.

Cream Cheese-Pepper Jelly Thumbprints

MAKES 3½ DOZEN
HANDS-ON 20 MINUTES TOTAL 3 HOURS, 20 MINUTES

This play on a traditional Southern appetizer has just enough of a savory element to be served before a meal. The pepper jelly can be replaced with a more kid-friendly option, such as strawberry jam, for a sweeter treat.

- ¾ cup butter, softened
- 4 ounces cream cheese, softened
- ½ cup sugar
- 1 large egg
- 1 teaspoon vanilla extract
- 2¼ cups all-purpose flour
- ¾ teaspoon baking powder
- ¼ teaspoon table salt
- Parchment paper
- ½ cup red or green pepper jelly

1. Beat first 3 ingredients at medium speed with an electric mixer 2 minutes or until light and fluffy. Beat in egg and vanilla until blended. Combine flour, baking powder, and salt; gradually add to butter mixture, beating at low speed until blended.

2. Shape dough into a 1-inch-thick disk. Wrap tightly in plastic wrap, and chill 2 to 24 hours.

3. Preheat oven to 350°F. Shape chilled dough into 1-inch balls. Place 1 inch apart on parchment paper-lined baking sheets. Press thumb into each ball, forming an indentation.

4. Bake at 350°F for 10 minutes. Remove from oven, and press indentations again, using the back of a spoon. Bake 8 to 10 more minutes or until edges are golden brown. Cool on baking sheets 5 minutes; transfer to a wire rack, and cool completely (about 20 minutes).

5. Spoon ½ teaspoon pepper jelly into each indentation.

Fresh Idea

Put your own stamp on these thumbprint cookies. Try fruit jelly, chocolate candies, lemon curd, or any filling that suits your fancy.

Peppermint Candy Cane Twists

MAKES 1½ DOZEN
HANDS-ON 20 MINUTES TOTAL 1 HOUR

Using sugar cookie mix reduces the prep time on these cute cookies. Omit the peppermint extract if your kids prefer.

Preheat oven to 375°F. Stir together 1 (16-ounce) package sugar cookie mix, ½ cup softened butter, ¼ cup all-purpose flour, 1 teaspoon peppermint extract, and 1 large egg until a dough forms. Divide dough in half; tint one half with red food coloring paste. Roll level tablespoonfuls of both doughs into 6-inch ropes. Twist 1 red rope with 1 white rope; pinch ends to seal. Place on parchment paper-lined baking sheets, curving one end to form a candy cane. Bake at 375°F for 9 to 11 minutes or until set. Cool completely on wire racks (about 20 minutes).

Gingerbread House Cutouts

MAKES 16 COOKIES
HANDS-ON 1 HOUR TOTAL 3 HOURS, 45 MINUTES

Bake these cookies for kids to decorate. Tint royal icing red and green, if desired.

1	cup firmly packed brown sugar
¾	cup butter, softened
½	cup molasses
1	large egg
3	cups all-purpose flour
1	teaspoon baking soda
2	teaspoons ground ginger
2	teaspoons ground cinnamon
½	teaspoon table salt
½	teaspoon ground cloves

Parchment paper
Easy Royal Icing
Garnishes: round gummy candies, hard peppermint candies, assorted sprinkles, bite-size licorice pieces, striped candy sticks

1. Beat brown sugar and butter at medium speed with an electric mixer 3 minutes or until light and fluffy. Beat in molasses and egg until well blended. Combine flour and next 5 ingredients; gradually add to sugar mixture, beating at low speed until blended. Divide dough in half, and shape into 2 flat disks; wrap in plastic wrap, and chill 2 hours or until firm.

2. Preheat oven to 350°F. Roll dough to ¼-inch thickness on a lightly floured surface. Use a knife and a ruler to cut dough into gingerbread house shapes that are about 4- to 5-inches tall and 3- to 4-inches wide, rerolling dough as needed. Place on parchment paper-lined baking sheets.

3. Bake at 350°F for 10 to 12 minutes or until set and edges are lightly browned. Cool on baking sheets 5 minutes; transfer to wire racks, and cool completely (about 20 minutes). Decorate as desired using Easy Royal Icing.

Easy Royal Icing

MAKES 2 CUPS
HANDS-ON 5 MINUTES TOTAL 5 MINUTES

Keep the icing covered so it doesn't dry out.

Beat 1 (16-ounce) package powdered sugar, ⅓ cup water, and ¼ cup meringue powder at medium speed with an electric mixer 2 minutes or until well blended and smooth.

Chai-Spiced Spritz Cookies

MAKES 7 DOZEN
HANDS-ON 20 MINUTES TOTAL 1 HOUR, 20 MINUTES

Be sure to use ungreased baking sheets (not lined with parchment paper). Otherwise, the dough won't release from the cookie press and adhere to the baking sheet.

1	cup butter, softened
1	cup powdered sugar
1	large egg
1	teaspoon vanilla extract
2	cups all-purpose flour
¾	teaspoon ground cinnamon
½	teaspoon table salt
½	teaspoon ground cardamom
½	teaspoon ground ginger
¼	teaspoon ground cloves
¼	teaspoon freshly ground black pepper

Sanding sugar

1. Preheat oven to 375°F. Beat butter and powdered sugar at medium speed with an electric mixer until light and fluffy. Beat in egg and vanilla. Combine flour and next 6 ingredients; gradually add to butter mixture, beating at low speed until blended.

2. Use a cookie press to shape dough into desired shapes, following manufacturer's instructions. Place on ungreased baking sheets. Sprinkle with sanding sugar.

3. Bake at 375°F for 10 to 12 minutes or until edges are lightly browned. Cool on baking sheets 5 minutes; transfer to wire racks, and cool completely (about 15 minutes).

Holiday Helper

Don't have a cookie press? Make slice-and-bake cookies instead. Divide dough in half, and shape each portion into a 7-inch log; wrap in plastic wrap, and chill 1 hour. Cut into ¼-inch slices, and bake as directed.

Dark Chocolate Crinkles

MAKES 2½ DOZEN
HANDS-ON 15 MINUTES TOTAL 1 HOUR, 30 MINUTES

These rich, chewy, brownie-like cookies will have the perfect crackled top if well coated in powdered sugar.

1	(4-ounce) bittersweet chocolate baking bar, chopped
⅓	cup granulated sugar
⅓	cup firmly packed dark brown sugar
¼	cup butter, softened
1	large egg
½	cup all-purpose flour
¼	cup unsweetened dark-process cocoa
1	teaspoon baking powder
⅛	teaspoon table salt
1	tablespoon coffee liqueur
1	cup powdered sugar

Parchment paper

1. Microwave chocolate in a small microwave-safe bowl at HIGH 1 to 1½ minutes or until melted and smooth, stirring at 30-second intervals. Cool 5 minutes.

2. Beat together granulated sugar and next 2 ingredients at medium speed with an electric mixer until light and fluffy; add egg, beating well. Beat in melted chocolate. Combine flour and next 3 ingredients; gradually add to sugar mixture, beating at low speed just until blended. Beat in coffee liqueur. Cover and chill dough 30 minutes.

3. Preheat oven to 350°F. Roll dough into 1-inch balls; roll balls in powdered sugar twice, letting balls stand 1 to 2 minutes in sugar between coatings. Place 2 inches apart on parchment paper-lined baking sheets.

4. Bake at 350°F for 12 to 14 minutes or until crackled and set. Cool on baking sheets 2 minutes; transfer to wire racks, and cool completely (about 20 minutes).

Ambrosia Macaroons

MAKES 4 DOZEN
HANDS-ON 15 MINUTES TOTAL 1 HOUR, 10 MINUTES

For a sweeter, more decadent cookie, dip the bottoms in melted white chocolate, or drizzle it over the top.

Preheat oven to 350°F. Combine 1 (14-ounce) package sweetened flaked coconut, 1 (14-ounce) can sweetened condensed milk, ½ cup chopped dried pineapple, 1 teaspoon vanilla extract, 1 teaspoon orange zest, and 1 teaspoon grapefruit zest. Beat 2 large egg whites and ¼ teaspoon table salt at medium speed with an electric mixer until stiff peaks form; fold into coconut mixture. Scoop mixture by level tablespoonfuls 1 inch apart on parchment paper-lined baking sheets. Bake at 350°F for 18 to 20 minutes or until golden brown. Cool completely on a wire rack (about 20 minutes).

Cookies for Santa (and his helpers!)

Guests should leave with as many cookies as they baked. If there are 8 guests, each should bake 8 dozen cookies from a single recipe. Then guests take home a dozen of each type of cookie, or wrap them to give. Offer a balance of recipes like (left to right): Santa's Favorite Cookies, Dark Chocolate Crinkles, Ambrosia Macaroons, Cranberry-Oatmeal Cookie Bark, Peppermint Candy Cane Twists, Chai-Spiced Spritz Cookies, Pecan Linzer Cookies, and Cream Cheese-Pepper Jelly Thumbprints.

Let It Snow!

Bring the dusting of (faux) snow inside. The wintry village beckons beyond the wreath-adorned door as guests depart with their homemade treats.

Lavish Welcome

Over-the-top mantel embellishments invite guests to an elegant evening of stargazing and socializing.

Dreamy White Christmas

Sticking to a simple, neutral palette of cream, gold, green, and gray is a soothing approach to holiday decorating that still makes a striking impression. Crisp white Polar Bear poinsettias brighten the firebox, no-fire-required, which is appreciated in warmer parts of the region, while cream stockings with a metallic abstract print add the expected sparkle. Packages, vases, and even the artwork above the mantel repeat the color theme. The focal point of the cocktail table is an arrangement of white ranunculus, brunia berries, star of Bethlehem, and silver dollar eucalyptus in a gilded trophy vase.

Mini Biscuits with Ham, White Cheddar, and Sweet Shallot Relish

SERVES 12
HANDS-ON 40 MINUTES TOTAL 2 HOURS, 10 MINUTES

These two-bite appetizers will disappear fast!

- 2 tablespoons butter
- 1½ cups finely chopped shallots
- 2 tablespoons brown sugar
- 3 tablespoons apple cider vinegar
- 1 tablespoon whole-grain mustard
- 3 cups self-rising flour
- ½ teaspoon baking powder
- ¼ teaspoon table salt
- ¼ cup cold shortening, cut into pieces
- ¼ cup cold butter, cut into pieces
- 1 cup cold buttermilk
- Parchment paper
- ¼ cup butter, softened
- 8 ounces thinly sliced ham, torn into 2-inch pieces
- 5 ounces sharp white Cheddar cheese, cut into 24 (⅛-inch-thick) squares

1. Melt 2 tablespoons butter in a medium skillet over medium heat. Add shallots, and cook, stirring often, 15 minutes or until beginning to caramelize. Add brown sugar, and cook 1 minute or until sugar is melted. Stir in vinegar and 2 tablespoons water.

2. Bring to a simmer; cook 2 minutes or until reduced and syrupy. Remove from heat; stir in mustard, and season with table salt and freshly ground pepper to taste. Cool completely (about 1 hour).

3. Preheat oven to 475°F. Combine flour, baking powder, and salt in a large bowl. Cut in shortening and ¼ cup cold butter with a pastry blender until coarse meal forms. Add buttermilk; stir with a fork until dry ingredients are moistened.

4. Turn dough out onto a lightly floured surface, and gently knead 3 or 4 times. Pat dough to ¾-inch thickness. Cut into 24 rounds, using a 1¾-inch round cutter, rerolling scraps once. Place dough rounds ½ inch apart on a parchment paper-lined baking sheet.

5. Bake at 475°F for 11 to 13 minutes or until golden brown. Transfer to a wire rack, and cool completely (about 15 minutes).

6. Cut biscuits in half horizontally; spread cut sides with ¼ cup softened butter. Top bottom halves of biscuits with ham, cheese, and shallot relish. Cover with biscuit tops.

Calvados-Bourbon Toddy

MAKES ABOUT 4 CUPS
HANDS-ON 5 MINUTES TOTAL 5 MINUTES

This is a warm and comforting drink with a pleasant aroma and flavor. Warm your mugs before filling with the cocktail by filling them with boiling water while you mix the drink together. Empty the mugs when you're ready to fill them with the cocktail.

- 1 cup bourbon
- 1 cup apple cider, warmed
- 1 cup boiling water
- ½ cup Calvados (French apple-flavored brandy)
- 2 tablespoons fresh lemon juice
- 2 tablespoons raw wildflower honey
- 4 cinnamon sticks
- Garnishes: lemon rind strips, cinnamon sticks

Combine all ingredients in a heatproof measuring cup. Pour through a wire-mesh strainer into 4 mugs.

Spiced Rosemary Dark and Stormy

SERVES 8
HANDS-ON 10 MINUTES TOTAL 10 MINUTES, PLUS 8 HOURS FOR STANDING

Inspired by the classic Dark and Stormy, this easy cocktail has a holiday spin with notes of allspice, ginger, and rosemary. The longer the rum is infused with rosemary, the stronger the flavor.

- 2 cups spiced rum
- 3 fresh rosemary sprigs
- 2 tablespoons Italian spiced liqueur, allspice dram, or other spiced liqueur
- ¼ cup fresh lime juice
- 4 cups ginger beer
- Garnish: fresh rosemary sprigs

1. Combine rum and rosemary in a 1-pint Mason jar. Seal jar; let stand 8 hours or up to 1 week.

2. Discard rosemary from infused rum. Combine infused rum, spiced liqueur, and lime juice.

3. Divide rum mixture among 8 tall glasses filled with ice. Top with ginger beer.

NOTE: We tested with Tuaca for Italian spiced liqueur.

Elderflower-Pomegranate Fizz

Look for St-Germain Elderflower liqueur for this recipe.

SERVES 8
HANDS-ON 5 MINUTES TOTAL 5 MINUTES

Stir together ¼ cup each pomegranate liqueur,
elderflower liqueur, lemon juice, and pomegranate
juice in a small pitcher. Divide among 8 chilled
Champagne flutes. Top with chilled dry sparkling
wine or Champagne. Garnish with pomegranate seeds.

Crab and Endive Spears with Salmon Roe

SERVES 10
HANDS-ON 25 MINUTES TOTAL 25 MINUTES

These stylish appetizers come together quickly without using the stove. Feel free to prep the crab salad ahead of time and assemble before guests arrive.

1   pound fresh lump crabmeat
⅓   cup crème fraîche
¼   cup finely chopped fennel
¼   cup finely chopped shallots
2   tablespoons finely chopped fresh chives
2   tablespoons finely chopped fresh flat-leaf parsley
1½   tablespoons lemon zest
3   tablespoons lemon juice
½   teaspoon table salt
½   teaspoon freshly ground black pepper
4   large heads Belgian endive
2   ounces fresh salmon roe
Garnishes: chopped fresh chives, chopped fennel fronds

1. Pick crabmeat, removing any bits of shell.

2. Stir together crème fraîche and next 8 ingredients in a bowl. Gently fold in crab.

3. Trim root ends from endive, and separate into spears. Arrange spears on a platter. Spoon crab salad onto wide ends of endive (about 2 tablespoons on each). Top with salmon roe.

Fresh Idea

If endive's bitter bite leaves you cold, steamed fresh artichoke leaves are a great stand-in. Plus, guests get a nice bit of artichoke in every bite.

Chilled Gazpacho Shooters

SERVES 12
HANDS-ON 20 MINUTES TOTAL 1 HOUR, 30 MINUTES

Roasted tomatoes add lots of flavor to this refreshing appetizer. The recipe yields enough for two (1-ounce) shooters each.

4   large vine-ripened tomatoes, halved and cored
2   tablespoons olive oil
½   teaspoon table salt
½   teaspoon black pepper
1   ounce rustic day-old bread, crusts removed
½   hothouse cucumber, peeled, seeded, and chopped
½   red bell pepper, chopped
¼   small white onion, chopped
2   garlic cloves, chopped
2   tablespoons fresh basil leaves
2   tablespoons high-quality sherry vinegar
Garnishes: olive oil, micro basil (or other micro greens), smoked paprika, chopped cucumber, chopped red bell pepper

1. Preheat oven to 425°F. Toss together tomatoes, 1 tablespoon oil, salt, and pepper in a bowl. Transfer to a baking sheet. Bake 30 minutes. Remove from oven, and cool to room temperature (about 30 minutes).

2. Peel tomatoes, and discard skins.

3. Combine bread and 1 cup water in a large bowl; let stand 10 minutes.

4. Add tomatoes and any accumulated juices, cucumber, and next 5 ingredients to bread mixture. Season with table salt and pepper to taste.

5. Process mixture, in batches, in a blender until smooth. Transfer to a bowl. Whisk in remaining 1 tablespoon oil, and season to taste. Chill until ready to serve. Serve chilled in tall shot glasses.

Oysters with Mignonette Trio

SERVES 12
HANDS-ON 20 MINUTES TOTAL 20 MINUTES,
NOT INCLUDING MIGNONETTES

Oysters on the half shell are a chic and interesting
cocktail-party treat. Served with a variety of
tart mignonette sauces makes them even better.

3   dozen oysters in the shell, shucked
Sparkling Rosé Mignonette
Chile-Cucumber Mignonette
Pickled Fennel Mignonette

Serve oysters on ice with mignonettes.

Sparkling Rosé Mignonette

MAKES ½ CUP
HANDS-ON 10 MINUTES TOTAL 40 MINUTES

¼   cup Champagne vinegar
1   small shallot, finely minced
¼   teaspoon kosher salt
¼   teaspoon freshly ground pepper
4   tablespoons sparkling rosé, chilled

Whisk together first 4 ingredients. Chill 30 minutes. Whisk in rosé before serving.

Chile-Cucumber Mignonette

MAKES ½ CUP
HANDS-ON 10 MINUTES TOTAL 40 MINUTES

¼   cup peeled, seeded, and finely chopped cucumber
1   red chile pepper, minced
1   shallot, finely minced
¼   teaspoon kosher salt
¼   teaspoon freshly ground pepper
2   tablespoons apple cider vinegar
3   tablespoons Champagne vinegar

Stir together all ingredients in a small bowl. Chill 30 minutes before serving. Serve chilled.

Pickled Fennel Mignonette

MAKES ¾ CUP
HANDS-ON 10 MINUTES TOTAL 40 MINUTES

¼   cup minced fennel bulb
2   tablespoons chopped fennel fronds
1   small shallot, finely minced
¼   teaspoon kosher salt
¼   teaspoon freshly ground black pepper
½   cup Champagne vinegar

Stir together all ingredients in a small bowl. Chill 30 minutes before serving. Serve chilled.

Herb-Dusted Potato Chips

SERVES 10
HANDS-ON **30 MINUTES** TOTAL **30 MINUTES**

The herb dust makes these chips unique and so flavorful. For giving, double or triple the recipe. Let the chips cool before packaging to send home with your guests.

1   teaspoon fine sea salt
1   teaspoon dried parsley
1   teaspoon dried dill
½   teaspoon garlic salt
½   teaspoon dried Italian seasoning
½   teaspoon dried oregano
¼   teaspoon freshly ground black pepper
2   medium-size Yukon gold potatoes (about 1¼ pounds)
Vegetable oil

1. Combine first 7 ingredients in a small bowl.

2. Cut potatoes into ⅟₁₆-inch-thick slices, using a mandoline.

3. Pour oil to depth of 4 inches into a Dutch oven; heat to 360°F. Fry potatoes in hot oil, in batches, 1 to 2 minutes or until golden brown, turning occasionally with a slotted spoon. Remove with a slotted spoon; drain on paper towels. Immediately sprinkle with herb mixture. Serve warm or at room temperature.

At Your Service

A well-stocked sideboard can be both decorative and utilitarian. Richly colored roses and fresh greenery are perfect floral accents, and dainty pink-and-gold teacups add glamorous detail to the serving platter.

Orange, Radish, and Butter Lettuce Salad

SERVES 12
HANDS-ON 20 MINUTES TOTAL 20 MINUTES

Combining bright and juicy winter citrus with a light vinaigrette and butter lettuce makes for an enticing start to your holiday meal.

6	navel oranges
1	tablespoon finely chopped shallots
1	tablespoon chopped fresh mint
2	teaspoons Dijon mustard
1	teaspoon honey
½	teaspoon orange zest
½	teaspoon kosher salt
¼	teaspoon freshly ground black pepper
2	tablespoons olive oil
2	tablespoons canola oil
6	cups frisée lettuce
2	medium-size heads butter lettuce, torn into bite-size pieces
2	bunches radishes, thinly sliced (about 3 cups)
½	cup chopped dry-roasted pistachios

1. Cut a ¼-inch-thick slice from each end of oranges, using a sharp, thin-bladed knife. Place fruit, cut sides down, on a cutting board. Peel fruit; cut away bitter white pith. Slice between membranes, and gently remove whole segments, holding fruit over a bowl to collect juices. Gently squeeze membranes to release any juice. Discard membranes. Reserve segments and juice (about 2 cups segments and ¾ cup juice).

2. Whisk together 6 tablespoons reserved orange juice, shallots, and next 6 ingredients in a bowl until blended. Whisk in both oils until well blended.

3. Add frisée, butter lettuce, and radishes; toss gently to coat. Top individual servings with orange segments. Sprinkle with pistachios.

Sea Salt-Poppy Seed Cloverleaf Rolls

MAKES 12 ROLLS
HANDS-ON 25 MINUTES TOTAL 2 HOURS, 15 MINUTES

There is nothing quite like freshly baked rolls, but if pushed for time, make these a day in advance and reheat just before serving. Wrap tightly in aluminum foil and store at room temperature.

1	cup warm milk (100° to 110°F)
1	(¼-ounce) envelope active dry yeast
2	tablespoons sugar
3	cups all-purpose flour
1¼	teaspoon table salt
6	tablespoons butter, melted
1	large egg, lightly beaten
1½	teaspoons poppy seeds
1½	teaspoons flaky sea salt

1. Stir together milk, yeast, and 1 tablespoon of the sugar in a 2-cup glass measuring cup; let stand 5 minutes.

2. Combine flour, table salt, and remaining 1 tablespoon sugar in bowl of a heavy-duty electric stand mixer; let stand 5 minutes. Add 4 tablespoons of the melted butter, egg, and yeast mixture; beat at low speed, using paddle attachment, 3 minutes or until blended and a soft, sticky dough forms. Increase speed to medium, attach dough hook, and beat 6 minutes or until dough is smooth and elastic but still slightly sticky. Cover bowl with plastic wrap, and let rise in a warm place (85°F), free from drafts, 1 hour or until doubled in bulk.

3. Punch dough down. Turn out onto a lightly floured surface. Divide dough into 12 equal portions (about 2 ounces each). Gently shape each portion into 3 (1¼-inch) balls; place in 12 buttered muffin cups. Brush tops of dough with remaining 2 tablespoons melted butter. Cover and let rise in a warm (85°F) place, free from drafts, 30 to 45 minutes or until doubled in bulk.

4. Preheat oven to 375°F. Sprinkle rolls with poppy seeds and sea salt.

5. Bake at 375°F for 15 to 17 minutes or until golden brown. Transfer to a wire rack. Serve warm or cool completely (about 30 minutes).

Orderly Flow

Organize the buffet for easy access but add lovely
details too. Blood oranges and fresh kumquats
are pretty garnishes that fit with the bright color
scheme, while candlelight adds glimmer.

Stuffed Beef Tenderloin

SERVES 12
HANDS-ON **30 MINUTES** TOTAL **1 HOUR, 15 MINUTES**

Stuffed beef tenderloin pairs well with a classic Béarnaise sauce for the perfect sumptuous holiday meal.

BEEF:
1   pound fresh Swiss chard, stemmed and chopped
2   tablespoons olive oil
2   garlic cloves, minced
½   teaspoon kosher salt
¼   teaspoon freshly ground black pepper
1   tablespoon butter
2   (4-ounce) packages exotic blend mushrooms, chopped
1   (5-pound) beef tenderloin, trimmed

RUB:
1   tablespoon kosher salt
1   tablespoon fennel seed, toasted and crushed
1   tablespoon chopped fresh rosemary
1   tablespoon freshly ground black pepper
5   garlic cloves, pressed
1   tablespoon olive oil

1. Prepare Beef: Preheat oven to 500°F. Cook Swiss chard in hot oil in a large nonstick skillet over medium-high heat, stirring constantly, until chard begins to wilt. Cook 1 minute or until completely wilted. Add minced garlic, ¼ teaspoon of the salt, and ⅛ teaspoon of the pepper; sauté 1 minute. Transfer to a bowl; let stand until cool enough to handle.

2. Gently squeeze excess moisture from cooked chard.

3. Melt butter in skillet over medium-high heat. Add mushrooms and remaining ¼ teaspoon salt and ⅛ teaspoon pepper. Cook, stirring occasionally, 8 minutes or until browned. Stir into chard.

4. Butterfly beef by making a lengthwise cut in 1 side, but not through the opposite side (leave about ½ inch); unfold. Flatten to a uniform thickness (about ¾ inch), using a rolling pin or flat side of a meat mallet. Sprinkle with salt and pepper. Spoon chard mixture down center of beef, leaving a ¼-inch border. Fold beef over chard, and tie with kitchen string at 2-inch intervals. Place beef, seam side down, on a lightly greased jelly-roll pan.

5. Prepare Rub: Stir together kosher salt and next 4 ingredients in a small bowl. Stir in oil to form a paste. Rub mixture over beef.

6. Bake at 500°F for 10 minutes. Reduce oven temperature to 350°F. Bake 20 to 25 minutes or until a meat thermometer inserted into thickest portion of tenderloin registers 130°F (rare). Let stand 15 minutes before slicing.

Béarnaise Sauce

MAKES 1¼ CUPS
HANDS-ON **15 MINUTES** TOTAL **15 MINUTES**

Classic Béarnaise Sauce is emulsified in the blender for an easy yet elegant sauce to accompany roasted beef tenderloin. If your béarnaise is too thick, gradually whisk in very hot water, 1 teaspoon at a time, until desired consistency is reached.

¼   cup Champagne vinegar
¼   cup dry white wine
2   tablespoons minced shallots
2   tablespoons chopped fresh tarragon
1   cup butter
3   large egg yolks
¼   teaspoon table salt
¼   teaspoon freshly ground black pepper
1   tablespoon hot water
1   teaspoon fresh lemon juice (optional)

1. Combine first 3 ingredients and 1 tablespoon of the tarragon in a small saucepan. Bring to a simmer over medium-high heat, and cook 3 minutes or until reduced to 2 tablespoons. Pour through a fine wire-mesh strainer into a blender. Discard solids. Let cool slightly.

2. Meanwhile, microwave butter in a microwave-safe bowl at HIGH 1 minute or until melted.

3. Place egg yolks in blender, and process until smooth. With blender running, add hot butter in a slow, steady stream, processing until smooth. Add salt, pepper, hot water, and, if desired, lemon juice. Process until blended.

4. Transfer to a bowl, and stir in remaining 1 tablespoon tarragon. Store at room temperature until ready to use (up to 1 hour).

Fennel-Potato Gratin

SERVES 12
HANDS-ON 45 MINUTES TOTAL 1 HOUR, 45 MINUTES

This gratin dish can be made one day ahead of time and reheated, covered with foil, in a 350°F oven for 30 minutes.

2   tablespoons butter
1   tablespoon olive oil
2   fennel bulbs (about 2¼ pounds), halved and thinly sliced crosswise (about ⅛-inch thick)
1   teaspoon kosher salt
½   teaspoon freshly ground black pepper
⅓   cup dry white wine
2½ pounds Yukon gold potatoes, peeled and cut into ⅛-inch-thick slices
3   garlic cloves, minced
3   cups heavy cream
2   cups (8 ounces) shredded Comté cheese

1. Preheat oven to 350°F. Melt butter with oil in a large skillet over medium heat. Add fennel, ½ teaspoon of the salt, and ¼ teaspoon of the pepper. Cook, stirring occasionally, 2 minutes. Add wine; cover, reduce heat to medium-low, and cook, stirring occasionally, 20 minutes or until fennel is tender.

2. Increase heat to medium-high, and cook, uncovered and stirring often, 7 to 8 minutes or until fennel is lightly browned.

3. Bring potatoes, garlic, cream, and remaining ½ teaspoon salt and ¼ teaspoon pepper to a low simmer in a Dutch oven over medium-high heat. Cover, reduce heat to medium-low, and simmer 10 minutes or until potatoes are almost tender.

4. Place one-third of potatoes in an even layer in a lightly greased 3-quart baking dish, using a slotted spoon. Sprinkle with ⅔ cup cheese. Top with half of fennel. Repeat layers once. Top with remaining potatoes and ⅔ cup cheese. Pour remaining cream mixture over top. Cover with aluminum foil.

5. Bake at 350°F for 20 minutes. Uncover and bake 30 to 35 minutes or until bubbly and golden brown. Let stand 10 minutes before serving.

Roasted Heirloom Root Vegetables in Lemon-Horseradish Butter

SERVES 12
HANDS-ON 20 MINUTES TOTAL 5 HOURS, 35 MINUTES

Roasting brings out the natural sweetness and earthiness of these beautiful root vegetables and is one of the easiest methods of cooking. Be sure your vegetables are uniform in size so they cook in the same amount of time. The compound butter makes enough to freeze for other uses, or even for holiday gift giving, such as with our Sea Salt-Poppy Seed Cloverleaf Rolls (page 86).

1   cup butter, softened
1   tablespoon chopped fresh thyme
1   tablespoon chopped fresh flat-leaf parsley
2   to 3 tablespoons freshly grated horseradish
1   teaspoon lemon zest
2   tablespoons fresh lemon juice
    Parchment or wax paper
2   pounds Chioggia beets, trimmed (about 6 medium)
2   pounds golden beets, trimmed (about 5 medium)
3   (6-ounce) packages fresh baby rainbow carrots, cut into 1-inch pieces
1   pound parsnips, cut into ¾-inch-thick slices
3   tablespoons extra virgin olive oil

1. Mash together first 6 ingredients in a medium bowl, using a fork.

2. Place butter mixture on a large piece of parchment or wax paper. Bring 1 side of paper over mixture. Hold down other end of paper. Place flat edge of a baking sheet or other sturdy flat object next to butter on paper. Using your other hand, hold end of baking sheet, and push bottom of baking sheet away from you into base of butter mixture, forming a 1½-inch-wide log. Chill 4 hours.

3. Meanwhile, preheat oven to 425°F. Cut all beets into ¾- to 1-inch wedges, if needed, for uniform pieces. Toss together beets, carrots, and next 2 ingredients in a large bowl. Season lightly with desired amount of kosher salt and freshly ground pepper, and toss. Place in a single layer on 2 large baking sheets, leaving space between vegetables.

4. Bake at 425°F for 1 hour and 15 minutes to 1½ hours or until tender and golden brown, stirring every 20 minutes.

5. Transfer roasted vegetables to a large bowl. Add ¼ cup butter mixture. Toss until well coated. Serve immediately with remaining butter mixture.

Festive Blooms

A fragrant floral arrangement featuring roses, tulips, and evergreens adds to the holiday spirit as guests take their seats and toast the occasion.

Grand Finale

Save room for dessert. Layers of classic coconut cake sandwich a rum-spiked eggnog filling for a sweet nod to the holiday.

Eggnog Coconut Cake

SERVES 12 TO 16
HANDS-ON 25 MINUTES TOTAL 7 HOURS, 5 MINUTES, NOT INCLUDING FROSTING AND FILLING

Two holiday classics—coconut cake and eggnog—come together in this dessert and the results couldn't be more delicious. The eggnog custard makes a great filling for tarts that have a gingersnap or graham cracker crust.

Parchment paper
1   cup unsalted butter, softened
1½   cups sugar
½   cup cream of coconut
1   teaspoon vanilla extract
4   large eggs
2¾   cups all-purpose flour
1   tablespoon baking powder
½   teaspoon table salt
1   cup unsweetened coconut milk
Eggnog Custard Filling
Whipped Cream Frosting
1½   cups unsweetened flaked coconut, toasted

1. Preheat oven to 350°F. Grease 2 (9-inch) round cake pans; line bottoms with parchment paper. Grease parchment; dust pans lightly with flour.

2. Beat butter and sugar at medium speed with a heavy-duty electric stand mixer until fluffy. Beat in cream of coconut and vanilla. Add eggs, one at a time, beating just until blended after each addition.

3. Whisk together flour, baking powder, and salt; add to butter mixture alternately with coconut milk, beginning and ending with flour mixture. Beat at low speed just until blended after each addition. Divide batter between prepared pans.

4. Bake at 350°F for 30 to 35 minutes or until a wooden pick inserted in center comes out clean. Cool in pans on wire racks 10 minutes; remove from pans to wire racks, and cool completely (about 1 hour).

5. Cut cake layers in half horizontally with a serrated knife. Place 1 cake layer on a serving plate or cake stand; spread with about ⅔ cup Eggnog Custard Filling. Repeat procedure twice; top with remaining cake layer. Spread Whipped Cream Frosting on top and sides of cake. Sprinkle flaked coconut around sides of cake. Cover and chill 4 to 24 hours. Let stand at room temperature at least 1 hour before serving.

NOTE: We tested with Coco Real for cream of coconut.

Eggnog Custard Filling

MAKES ABOUT 2 CUPS
HANDS-ON 15 MINUTES TOTAL 2 HOURS, 15 MINUTES

1⅓   cups eggnog
⅓   cup milk
3   tablespoons sugar
2   tablespoons cornstarch
¼   teaspoon freshly ground nutmeg
⅛   teaspoon table salt
3   large egg yolks
1   tablespoon dark rum

1. Whisk together first 7 ingredients in a heavy saucepan. Bring to a boil over medium heat, whisking constantly. Boil, whisking constantly, 1 minute or until thickened. Remove from heat; whisk in rum.

2. Pour mixture into a bowl. Place heavy-duty plastic wrap directly on warm custard (to prevent a film from forming); chill 2 to 8 hours.

Whipped Cream Frosting

MAKES ABOUT 4 CUPS
HANDS-ON 5 MINUTES TOTAL 5 MINUTES

2   cups heavy cream
¼   cup powdered sugar
1½   tablespoons dark rum
½   teaspoon vanilla extract

Beat heavy cream, powdered sugar, dark rum, and vanilla extract at medium speed with an electric mixer until stiff peaks form.

Holiday Helper

Need to bake and take to a party? Insert toothpicks into the top and sides of the frosted cake and drape with plastic wrap to keep cake covered and toppings in place.

Savor

No-Cook
Appetizers

Relax by the fire. Don't slave by a stove. Entertaining is stress free when no cooking is required. Yes, really!

Herbed Feta and Sun-Dried Tomato Dip

SERVES 10
HANDS-ON 15 MINUTES TOTAL 15 MINUTES

Serve with crackers or crudités for an addictive dip. It's also a perfect accompaniment to cocktails.

1   (6-ounce) container crumbled feta cheese
6   ounces cream cheese, softened
½   cup sun-dried tomatoes in oil
⅓   cup mayonnaise
⅓   cup sour cream
¼   cup firmly packed fresh basil leaves, coarsely chopped
1   tablespoon chopped fresh dill
1   teaspoon lemon zest
1   garlic clove, minced
¼   teaspoon crushed red pepper
¼   teaspoon freshly ground black pepper

Process all ingredients in a food processor 10 to 15 seconds or until blended.

Fresh Idea

Think beyond the carrot and celery sticks when it comes to raw veggies for dips and spreads. Whole, shaved, or sliced, a rainbow of tasty options are worth seeking out—red, purple, or yellow radishes; fennel; green onions; raw beets (yellow varieties don't stain fingers); Romanesco, cauliflower, and broccoli; asparagus; snap peas; and the tender inner leaves of butter lettuce, radicchio, and endive all add color and deliciousness to any holiday crudité platter.

Pistachio-Crusted Goat Cheese Log

SERVES 12 TO 16
HANDS-ON 10 MINUTES TOTAL 4 HOURS, 10 MINUTES

Accented with dried apricots and thyme, this goat cheese log is very savory with a hint of sweetness. Serve with assorted crackers and crostini.

1   (8-ounce) block cream cheese, softened
1   (8-ounce) log goat cheese, softened
½   cup finely chopped dried apricots
3   tablespoons finely chopped green onions
2   teaspoons chopped fresh thyme
½   teaspoon fine sea salt
¼   teaspoon freshly ground black pepper
¾   cup roasted, salted pistachios, chopped

1. Beat cream cheese and goat cheese with an electric mixer until smooth; beat in apricots and next 4 ingredients until well blended.

2. Turn mixture out onto a large piece of plastic wrap; use plastic wrap to shape into an 8- x 2-inch log. Wrap in plastic wrap, and chill 4 hours or until firm.

3. Unwrap cheese log; roll in pistachios to coat. Serve immediately, or chill, wrapped in plastic wrap, until ready to serve.

Cheese and Almond Fig Bites

SERVES 24
HANDS-ON 10 MINUTES TOTAL 10 MINUTES

These sweet and savory bites are packed with flavor; serve on top of table water crackers, if desired. Look for dried figs in the produce section sold in a tray; they are the best quality and are more tender.

24 dried Mission figs
1 (5.2-ounce) package spreadable cheese with black pepper
Marcona almonds
Wildflower honey (optional)
Garnish: fresh basil leaves

Top each fig with about 1 teaspoon cheese and 2 or 3 almonds. Drizzle with honey, if desired.

NOTE: We tested with Orchard Choice Mission figs and Boursin spreadable cheese.

Prosciutto-Caprese Skewers

SERVES 16
HANDS-ON 15 MINUTES TOTAL 15 MINUTES

Reminiscent of snowmen...only much tastier.

Thread small mozzarella cheese balls (from 1 [¾-pound] package, such as ciliegini) onto 3-inch skewers or wooden picks. Tear thinly sliced prosciutto (from 1 [4-ounce] package) into 4 pieces each, and thread onto skewers. Thread 1 cherry tomato (from 1 [10.5-ounce] package) onto each skewer. Stir together 8 teaspoons basil pesto and 2 teaspoons extra virgin olive oil, and drizzle over skewers. Serve at room temperature.

Marinated Burrata

SERVES 6
HANDS-ON 10 MINUTES TOTAL 8 HOURS, 10 MINUTES

Whisk together ¼ cup olive oil, 1 minced red chile pepper, 2 tablespoons chopped fresh basil, 1 teaspoon lemon zest, 1½ teaspoons table salt, and ½ teaspoon pepper in a bowl. Carefully place 2 (8-ounce) balls burrata cheese in an 11- x 7-inch baking dish, and top with olive oil mixture. Cover and chill at least 8 hours or up to 24 hours. Carefully transfer to a small platter, and serve with crackers. Garnish with fresh basil leaves, if desired.

Smoked Salmon Spread

MAKES 3 CUPS
HANDS-ON 15 MINUTES TOTAL 15 MINUTES

This spread is excellent on bagels for Christmas brunch or with drinks for a pre-dinner appetizer served with bagel chips or water crackers. We tested with Nova lox, which has a bright pink color.

12   ounces cream cheese, softened
8   ounces cold-smoked salmon, torn into pieces
½   cup sour cream
2   tablespoons finely diced red onion
1   tablespoon fresh lemon juice
1   tablespoon capers, drained
1   tablespoon chopped fresh dill
½   teaspoon freshly ground black pepper

Process cream cheese, salmon, sour cream, 1 tablespoon of the red onion, lemon juice, capers, 1 teaspoon of the dill, and pepper in a food processor until a coarse puree forms. Season to taste with salt. Transfer spread to a small serving bowl. Sprinkle with remaining 2 teaspoons fresh dill and 1 tablespoon red onion.

Radish, Olive, and Herb Butter Tartines

SERVES 10
HANDS-ON 15 MINUTES TOTAL 15 MINUTES

A classic French snack of radishes and butter gets an upgrade with a herb-and-olive flavor infusion.

½   cup unsalted butter, softened
2   tablespoons chopped fresh parsley
2   tablespoons chopped fresh chives
1   tablespoon pitted kalamata olives, chopped
2   teaspoons chopped fresh dill
1   small garlic clove, chopped
½   teaspoon kosher salt
½   teaspoon black pepper
1   French bread baguette, cut diagonally into ½-inch-thick slices
6   medium radishes, very thinly sliced
Garnishes: flaky sea salt, fresh herbs

Pulse first 8 ingredients in a food processor until blended but not smooth (about 20 [1-second] pulses), scraping sides of bowl as needed. Spread 1 to 1½ teaspoons herb butter over 1 side of each bread slice, and top with radishes.

Fresh Idea

Round out your holiday nibbles with fresh picks made by Southern artisans or wrap some up as favors so your guests can take home a genuine taste of the South. Some of our favorites to seek out:

• Wickles Wicked Okra of Dadeville, Alabama (wicklespickles.com)
• Texas Sweet Heat Pickles of Austin, Texas (poguemahonepickles.com)
• Green Martini Mater Pickles of Winston-Salem, North Carolina (betaverde.blogspot.com)
• Olli Salumeria Salami, slow-cured in Virginia and available at specialty grocers throughout the South
• Neita's Charleston Vinaigrettes and Marinades of Charleston, South Carolina (neitasvinaigrettes.com)
• Pork Clouds pork skins from Atlanta, Georgia, come in an array of inspired flavors (baconsheir.com)

Horseradish and Roast Beef Crostini

SERVES 15
HANDS-ON 15 MINUTES TOTAL 15 MINUTES

*Make your own crostini, if desired, using
a French baguette from the deli, or purchase
store-bought crostini for a fast and easy option.
You may need to cut the roast beef in half crosswise
to fit, depending on the size of your crostini.*

- ½ cup crème fraîche (or sour cream)
- 1 tablespoon prepared horseradish
- ⅛ teaspoon table salt
- ⅛ teaspoon freshly ground black pepper
- 30 store-bought or homemade crostini toasts
- 8 ounces premium thinly sliced deli-roasted roast beef
- 1 (2-ounce) package fresh watercress

1. Stir together crème fraîche, horseradish, salt,
and pepper.

2. Spread one side of each crostini with crème fraîche
mixture. Top with roast beef and watercress.

Sopressata, Smoked Gouda, and Apple Canapés with Balsamic Mustard

SERVES 20
HANDS-ON 20 MINUTES TOTAL 20 MINUTES

This is a great dish for any friends who are gluten free.

¼ cup balsamic glaze

1 tablespoon whole-grain Dijon mustard

2 medium-size Granny Smith or Gala apples, cut crosswise into 10 (¼-inch-thick) slices

1 medium lemon, halved

8 ounces smoked Gouda cheese, cut into ¹⁄₁₆-inch-thick slices

8 ounces thinly sliced Italian salami (such as sopressata)

1. Stir together balsamic glaze and mustard in a small bowl.

2. Rub apple slices with lemon halves. Top each apple slice with 1 slice cheese and 2 slices salami. Drizzle with glaze mixture.

NOTE: We tested with 2 (4-ounce) packages of Boar's Head sliced sopressata.

Zesty Marinated Shrimp

SERVES 12
HANDS-ON 10 MINUTES TOTAL 8 HOURS, 10 MINUTES

This new-school spin on an old-school Southern favorite gets a bit of kick from crushed red pepper and brightness from lemon zest and fresh herbs. Most supermarkets sell cooked, peeled shrimp, but visit your local seafood market for the best quality.

1½	pounds peeled, medium-size cooked shrimp
1½	cups thinly sliced red onion
½	cup extra virgin olive oil
⅓	cup red wine vinegar
2	tablespoons chopped fresh flat-leaf parsley
2	tablespoons chopped fresh dill
3	tablespoons drained capers
1	teaspoon lemon zest
3	tablespoons fresh lemon juice
1	teaspoon kosher salt
½	teaspoon crushed red pepper
2	garlic cloves, thinly sliced

Combine all ingredients in a large zip-top plastic freezer bag. Seal and chill 8 to 24 hours, turning occasionally.

Halibut Ceviche with Avocado and Lime

MAKES 2½ CUPS
HANDS-ON 10 MINUTES TOTAL 30 MINUTES

This ceviche is super refreshing thanks to fresh cilantro and lime. Serve with store-bought deep-fried wonton wrappers.

1	pound very fresh halibut (or similar firm, white fish), cut into ½-inch pieces
1	avocado, diced
2	small shallots, cut into rings
7	tablespoons fresh lime juice
¼	cup coarsely chopped fresh cilantro
1	small jalapeño pepper, seeded and minced
1¼	teaspoons kosher salt

Combine all ingredients in a bowl, and let stand at room temperature until fish is opaque (about 20 to 30 minutes).

Arugula and Watercress Salad with Fennel and Smoked Trout on Crackers

SERVES 24
HANDS-ON 15 MINUTES TOTAL 15 MINUTES

Fennel's sweet licorice flavor tempers the strong, sharp flavors of smoked trout and peppery greens.

1	tablespoon chopped fresh dill
1	tablespoon finely chopped fresh chives
2	tablespoons Champagne vinegar
2	tablespoons extra virgin olive oil
1	tablespoon sour cream
¾	teaspoon kosher salt
½	teaspoon freshly ground black pepper
3	cups firmly packed arugula
3	cups firmly packed watercress
½	large fennel bulb, shaved
4	ounces smoked trout, coarsely flaked
2	(4.25-ounce) boxes table water crackers

Garnishes: fennel fronds, chopped fresh dill, finely chopped fresh chives

1. Whisk together first 7 ingredients.

2. Toss together arugula, watercress, and fennel in a large bowl, and drizzle with ¼ cup dressing. Add more dressing, if desired. Toss to coat. Add trout, and toss gently until blended.

3. Top each cracker with 1 tablespoon salad mixture.

Fresh Idea

Don't feel wedded to a recipe. If you prefer crawfish tail meat to shrimp, grouper to halibut, or smoked shredded pork over smoked trout, make swaps to suit your taste. Recipes are templates for tinkering.

Southern
Sides

Side dishes in the South are rarely afterthoughts and often are the fought-over stars of the table. These recipes are no exception.

Roasted Brussels Sprouts with Lemon Brown Butter and Hazelnuts

SERVES 8
HANDS-ON 20 MINUTES TOTAL 45 MINUTES

Sumptuous brown butter with a touch of lemon cloaks tender roasted Brussels sprouts. Topped with crunchy, earthy, toasted hazelnuts, this side dish may steal the show!

2   pounds Brussels sprouts
2   tablespoons olive oil
¾   teaspoon kosher salt
½   teaspoon freshly ground black pepper
6   tablespoons unsalted butter
1   teaspoon lemon zest
¼   cup fresh lemon juice
½   cup chopped toasted hazelnuts

1. Preheat oven to 400°F. Trim ends of Brussels sprouts, and remove outer leaves. Cut any large Brussels sprouts in half lengthwise (through stem and bottom ends). Place on a large jelly-roll pan; drizzle with oil, and sprinkle with ½ teaspoon of the salt and pepper. Toss gently.

2. Bake at 400°F for 25 minutes or until tender and lightly browned, stirring after 10 minutes.

3. Meanwhile, cook butter in a medium skillet over medium-high heat, whisking constantly, 5 minutes or until fragrant and deep golden brown (do not burn). Whisk in lemon zest and juice.

4. Toss Brussels sprouts with browned butter mixture and remaining ¼ teaspoon salt in a large bowl. Sprinkle with hazelnuts, and serve immediately.

Sweet Corn and Poblano Pudding

SERVES 10 TO 12
HANDS-ON 20 MINUTES TOTAL 55 MINUTES

Most Southerners are bound to have "put up" frozen corn from their summer gardens, and, by all means, use it in this casserole. However, frozen corn from the Piggly Wiggly will do just fine too.

2   tablespoons butter
1   cup chopped sweet onion
1   cup chopped red bell pepper
1   cup chopped poblano pepper
4   cups frozen corn kernels, thawed
5   large eggs
1   cup heavy cream
¾   cup half-and-half
¼   cup chopped fresh parsley
¼   cup chopped fresh cilantro
1   tablespoon hot sauce
1   tablespoon Worcestershire sauce
½   teaspoon ground cumin
2   cups (8 ounces) shredded white Cheddar cheese
1   cup crushed tortilla chips

1. Preheat oven to 350°F. Melt butter in a large skillet over medium high heat. Add onion and both peppers; cook 4 minutes or until softened. Add corn, and cook 3 minutes. Remove from heat, and cool slightly.

2. Whisk together eggs and next 7 ingredients in a bowl until blended. Stir in vegetables and cheese. Pour mixture into a 13- x 9-inch baking dish coated with cooking spray.

3. Bake at 350°F for 30 to 35 minutes. Sprinkle with chips, and bake 5 more minutes or until golden brown and set.

Caramelized Carrots with Hazelnut Gremolata

SERVES 8
HANDS-ON 15 MINUTES TOTAL 25 MINUTES

This colorful side is the perfect complement to roasted meats, providing sweetness and crunch. Toast hazelnuts in a skillet over medium-low heat until fragrant.

¼   cup hazelnuts, toasted and chopped
3   tablespoons fresh flat-leaf parsley leaves, chopped
1   teaspoon lemon zest
1   teaspoon fresh lemon juice
1   pound carrots, cut into 3- to 4-inch-long (½-inch-thick) pieces
2   tablespoons unsalted butter
1   tablespoon maple syrup
1   teaspoon kosher salt
½   teaspoon black pepper

1. Stir together first 4 ingredients in a small bowl.

2. Bring carrots and ½ cup water to a boil in a large saucepan, covered, over high heat. Boil 5 minutes. Uncover and cook until liquid evaporates (about 1 minute). Decrease heat to medium.

3. Add butter, syrup, salt and pepper. Cook, stirring occasionally, 4 minutes or until edges of carrots are caramelized and lightly brown. Transfer carrots to a serving platter, and sprinkle with hazelnut gremolata.

Oven-Roasted Haricots Verts with Blistered Tomatoes and Olives

SERVES 6 TO 8
HANDS-ON 10 MINUTES TOTAL 35 MINUTES

Roasting transforms year-round ingredients into extraordinary accents.

2	pounds haricots verts (French green beans)
2	(10-ounce) containers grape or cherry tomatoes
3	large shallots, thinly sliced
¼	cup olive oil
2	tablespoons chopped fresh thyme
1½	tablespoons chopped fresh oregano
1½	teaspoons kosher salt
½	teaspoon freshly ground black pepper
⅓	cup chopped pitted kalamata olives
1	tablespoon chopped fresh parsley

1. Preheat oven to 425°F. Toss together first 8 ingredients in a large bowl. Divide between 2 large jelly-roll pans.

2. Bake at 425°F for 25 to 30 minutes or until beans are tender and tomatoes burst, rotating pans after 15 minutes.

3. Transfer to a platter; top with olives and parsley. Serve hot or at room temperature.

Creamy Kabocha Squash-Parsnip Mash

SERVES 8
HANDS-ON 30 MINUTES TOTAL 1 HOUR, 30 MINUTES

Also called Japanese pumpkin, kabocha squash's earthiness marries beautifully with the sweetness of parsnips and cream.

6	to 8 pound kabocha squash, halved and seeded
2	tablespoons unsalted butter, melted
1	tablespoon kosher salt
2	teaspoons freshly ground black pepper
1	pound parsnips, peeled and cut into 1-inch pieces
2	cups heavy cream
½	cup chicken broth
4	fresh thyme sprigs
3	garlic cloves, smashed
1	bay leaf

1. Preheat oven to 450°F. Brush cut sides of squash with butter, and sprinkle with 2 teaspoons of the salt and 1 teaspoon of the pepper. Place, cut sides down, on a large jelly-roll pan.

2. Bake at 450°F for 35 to 40 minutes or until tender when pierced with a fork and pulp is easily scooped from skin. Cool on pan 15 minutes.

3. Scrape out pulp from squash into a bowl, and mash with a potato masher until smooth.

4. Bring parsnips, next 5 ingredients, and remaining 1 teaspoon salt and 1 teaspoon pepper to a boil in a saucepan over medium heat. Reduce heat, and simmer, covered, 15 to 20 minutes or until parsnips are very tender. Pour through a strainer into a bowl, reserving liquid; discard thyme sprigs, garlic, and bay leaf.

5. Pulse squash pulp and parsnips in a food processor, adding enough reserved liquid, 2 tablespoons at a time, to reach desired consistency. Season with salt and pepper to taste.

Baby Kale and Pears with Roasted Shallot Vinaigrette

SERVES 8
HANDS-ON 15 MINUTES TOTAL 45 MINUTES

Tender baby kale leaves dressed in a savory, rich, roasted shallot dressing are enhanced by the sweetness of fall pears in this festive first course. Use a vegetable peeler to get pretty curls of cheese to garnish each plate of dressed salad.

4	large shallots, halved
½	cup olive oil
1	large fresh thyme sprig
¼	cup high-quality sherry vinegar
1	tablespoon chopped fresh thyme
1	tablespoon Dijon mustard
1	tablespoon honey
1	teaspoon kosher salt
¼	teaspoon freshly ground black pepper
4	medium-size, ripe Bosc pears, thinly sliced
2	(5-ounce) packages mixed greens with baby kale
1	cup toasted pecan halves
4	ounces Parmigiano-Reggiano cheese, shaved

1. Preheat oven to 375°F. Place shallots, oil, and thyme sprig in a small baking dish. Cover loosely with aluminum foil. Bake 30 minutes or until shallots are light golden brown and very tender. Discard thyme sprig.

2. Pulse roasted shallot mixture, vinegar, chopped thyme, mustard, honey, ¾ teaspoon of the salt, and pepper in a blender until shallots are mashed. Process until blended, scraping down sides as needed.

3. Toss pears with ¼ cup dressing in a bowl.

4. Toss mixed greens with ¼ cup dressing in a large bowl, and sprinkle with remaining ¼ teaspoon salt. Transfer greens to a large platter, top with pears, and sprinkle with pecans and cheese.

NOTE: To make ahead, prepare recipe as directed through Step 3 up to 1 hour ahead. Store pears and dressing in refrigerator. Proceed with recipe as directed in Step 4 when ready to serve.

Grits and Greens Casserole

SERVES 10 TO 12
HANDS-ON 25 MINUTES TOTAL 1 HOUR, 10 MINUTES

This rich and creamy grits casserole is as delicious alongside eggs and brunch dishes as it is with roasted meats and vegetables at your holiday dinner. Serve with your favorite hot sauce or pepper vinegar for authentic Southern flavor.

- 10 ounces country ham slices, chopped (about 2 cups chopped)
- 2 tablespoons olive oil
- 1 tablespoon chopped garlic
- 6 cups chicken broth
- 2 cups half-and-half
- 2 cups uncooked stone-ground grits
- ½ cup unsalted butter
- 1 cup (4 ounces) shredded sharp white Cheddar cheese
- 1 (9-ounce) package baby kale, lightly chopped
- 1½ cups panko (Japanese breadcrumbs)
- ½ cup grated Parmesan cheese
- ½ teaspoon freshly ground black pepper

1. Preheat oven to 350°F. Cook ham in hot oil in a Dutch oven over medium heat, stirring often, 10 to 12 minutes or until lightly browned (reduce heat, if needed). Add garlic, and cook, stirring often, 1 minute. Add broth, and stir, scraping bottom of Dutch oven to remove browned bits.

2. Increase heat to medium-high, add half-and-half, and bring to a low boil. Stir in grits. Cook over medium heat, stirring often, 20 minutes or until grits are tender and creamy. Add 6 tablespoons of the butter. Stir in Cheddar cheese and kale, stirring until cheese and butter are melted and kale is wilted.

3. Coat a 13- x 9-inch baking dish with cooking spray. Spoon grits mixture into prepared dish.

4. Melt remaining 2 tablespoons butter in a bowl. Add panko, Parmesan cheese, and pepper, and toss to coat. Sprinkle over grits mixture.

5. Bake at 350°F for 15 to 20 minutes or until thoroughly heated and topping is golden brown. Serve immediately.

NOTE: We tested with McEwen & Sons grits.

Lemon-Roasted Turnips with Bacon and Thyme

SERVES 8 TO 10
HANDS-ON 20 MINUTES TOTAL 1 HOUR

The earthy flavor of roasted turnips and bacon is enhanced by the sweet and sour combination of ingredients in this dish. Served alongside your favorite holiday meats, this will surely delight your dinner guests. If you can't find sorghum, use honey, though sorghum is preferred.

Parchment paper
½   pound thick-cut bacon slices, chopped
3   pounds turnips, cut into ½-inch wedges
1   large sweet onion, sliced
2   tablespoons olive oil
1   tablespoon apple cider vinegar
1   tablespoon sorghum
2   teaspoons lemon zest
1   tablespoon chopped fresh thyme
1   teaspoon fresh lemon juice
Table salt and freshly ground black pepper
Lemon wedges

1. Preheat oven to 475°F. Line 2 large jelly-roll pans with parchment paper.

2. Cook bacon in a large skillet over medium-high heat 8 to 10 minutes or until crisp. Remove bacon with a slotted spoon, and drain on paper towels, reserving 2 tablespoons drippings in a large bowl.

3. Stir turnips and next 5 ingredients into drippings in bowl. Place in a single layer on prepared pans.

4. Bake at 475°F for 40 to 45 minutes or until golden brown and tender, rotating and turning baking sheets halfway through. Remove from oven, and sprinkle with thyme, lemon juice, and bacon. Season with salt and pepper to taste. Serve immediately with lemon wedges.

Butter Bean Gratin with Herbed Cornbread Crust

SERVES 10 TO 12
HANDS-ON 30 MINUTES TOTAL 2 HOURS, 10 MINUTES

Sometimes we Southerners have the presence of mind to store away the bounty of summer gardens and "put up" some butter beans in our freezers. The holidays are a perfect time to enjoy distant memories of fresh peas and beans, and this is a perfect way to present them, complete with a crust made of crunchy herbed cornbread.

BEANS:

6	bacon slices
1	cup diced sweet onion
1	shallot, chopped
3	cups chicken broth
3	cups heavy cream
1	bay leaf
3	tablespoons chopped fresh chives
1	tablespoon chopped fresh thyme
1	teaspoon lemon zest

Table salt and freshly ground black pepper to taste

6	cups fresh baby butter beans*

TOPPING:

1½	cups buttermilk
1	cup plain yellow cornmeal
½	cup all-purpose flour
½	cup (2 ounces) shredded Parmesan cheese
¼	cup canola oil
2	tablespoons chopped fresh parsley
1½	teaspoons baking powder
1	teaspoon baking soda
½	teaspoon table salt
1	large egg, lightly beaten

1. Prepare Beans: Preheat oven to 400°F. Cook bacon in a large, deep skillet or Dutch oven over medium heat 6 to 8 minutes or until crisp. Drain bacon on a paper towel-lined plate, reserving 2 tablespoons drippings in skillet. Increase heat to medium high. Crumble or chop bacon.

2. Sauté onion and shallot in hot drippings 4 to 5 minutes or until softened. Add broth, cream, and bay leaf, and bring to a boil. Stir in 1 tablespoon of the chives, thyme, and lemon zest. Season with salt and pepper to taste, and remove from heat.

3. Place butter beans in a lightly greased 13- x 9-inch baking dish; pour hot cream mixture over beans. Place baking dish on a jelly-roll pan.

4. Bake at 400°F for 1 hour and 20 minutes or until sauce is thickened.

5. Meanwhile, prepare Topping: Stir together buttermilk, next 9 ingredients, reserved bacon, and remaining 2 tablespoons chives in a medium bowl until blended. (Prepare the topping just as the beans are finished baking.)

6. Spoon cornmeal mixture over bean mixture, smoothing to cover entire surface evenly.

7. Bake 20 minutes or until golden brown.

*5 (10-ounce) packages frozen baby limas, thawed, may be substituted.

Wilted Chard with Salami Crumbs

SERVES 6
HANDS-ON 25 MINUTES TOTAL 25 MINUTES

Feel free to swap out the salami for pancetta or bacon, and the chard for kale or collards. We tested with sopressata salami.

1	cup chopped Italian dried salami (about 4 ounces)
2	tablespoons extra virgin olive oil
3	garlic cloves, minced
¼	teaspoon crushed red pepper
½	cup panko (Japanese breadcrumbs)
1¾	pounds Swiss chard, coarsely chopped
1	tablespoon sherry vinegar
1	teaspoon kosher salt
½	teaspoon freshly ground black pepper

1. Sauté salami in 1 tablespoon hot oil in a large skillet over medium heat 6 to 8 minutes or until crisp. Add garlic and red pepper, and sauté 1 minute. Add panko, and cook 3 minutes or until just beginning to brown. Transfer to a bowl.

2. Heat remaining 1 tablespoon oil in skillet over medium-high heat. Add chard, and cook 4 minutes or just until wilted, stirring with tongs. Drizzle with vinegar, salt, and pepper, and transfer to a platter. Sprinkle with breadcrumb mixture.

Savory Sweet Potato Casserole

SERVES 10 TO 12
HANDS-ON 15 MINUTES TOTAL 1 HOUR, 40 MINUTES

This savory take on the classic super-sweet standard will be a welcome addition to your holiday menu. Use your time wisely and bake the sweet potatoes ahead. You can even put the casserole together a day or two ahead of time (wait to sprinkle the topping on just before baking).

- 4 pounds sweet potatoes
- 2 (5.2-ounce) packages garlic-and-herb spreadable cheese
- ½ teaspoon kosher salt
- ¼ teaspoon freshly ground pepper
- 3 large eggs
- 2 tablespoons butter, melted
- ¾ cup chopped pecans
- ¾ cup panko (Japanese breadcrumbs)
- ¼ cup shaved Parmesan cheese
- 2 tablespoons chopped fresh parsley

1. Preheat oven to 400°F. Place sweet potatoes on a baking sheet. Bake 1 hour or until tender. Cool slightly, and peel.

2. Place sweet potato flesh in a medium bowl. Beat together sweet potato flesh, cheese, salt, and pepper until smooth, using a hand mixer with a whisk attachment. Beat in eggs, one at a time, until blended. Spoon sweet potato mixture into a 13- x 9-inch baking dish coated with cooking spray.

3. Stir together butter, pecans, panko, Parmesan, and parsley in a bowl. Sprinkle mixture over sweet potato mixture.

4. Bake at 400°F for 20 minutes or until puffed and golden. Let stand 5 to 10 minutes before serving.

Upper-Crust
Comforts

Crunchy, crusty, crispy toppings make main dishes,
side dishes, and desserts downright swoon-worthy.

Iron Skillet Tamale Pie

SERVES 8 TO 10
HANDS-ON 35 MINUTES TOTAL 55 MINUTES

Not to be confused with authentic Mexican tamales, this American invention is essentially thick chili topped with a cornbread crust. What could be more comforting than that? It's a perfect low-key family meal for a winter evening. You may want to place a baking sheet on the oven rack below the skillet to catch any drips. To save time, use a bag of cornbread mix instead of making the homemade cornbread topping.

FILLING:

1½	pounds ground chuck
1	medium onion, chopped
2	poblano peppers, chopped
3	garlic cloves, minced
2	tablespoons ancho chili powder
1	tablespoon ground cumin
1	teaspoon dried oregano
2	(14.5-ounce) cans fire-roasted diced tomatoes
1	(16-ounce) can red chili beans in medium sauce
1	cup beef broth
1	cup frozen whole kernel corn, thawed
3	tablespoons chopped fresh cilantro

CORNBREAD TOPPING:

1¼	cups stone-ground yellow cornmeal
1	cup (4 ounces) shredded extra-sharp Cheddar cheese
¾	cup all-purpose flour
1	teaspoon baking soda
1	teaspoon baking powder
1	teaspoon table salt
¼	teaspoon freshly ground black pepper
1¼	cups buttermilk
¼	cup butter, melted
2	large eggs

SERVE WITH:

Sour cream
Sliced green onions

1. Prepare Filling: Preheat oven to 425°F. Cook ground beef, onion, poblanos, and garlic in a 12-inch cast-iron skillet 8 to 10 minutes or until meat crumbles and is no longer pink and onions are tender. Stir in ancho chili powder, cumin, and oregano; cook 2 minutes. Stir in tomatoes and next 3 ingredients; bring to a simmer. Reduce heat, and simmer 10 minutes or until slightly thickened. Stir in cilantro and salt and pepper to taste.

2. Meanwhile, prepare Cornbread Topping: Combine cornmeal and next 6 ingredients in a large bowl. Whisk together buttermilk, butter, and eggs; add to dry ingredients, stirring just until moistened. Dollop batter over mixture in skillet; spread into an even layer.

3. Bake at 425°F for 20 minutes or until golden brown and a wooden pick inserted in center of cornbread comes out clean. Serve with sour cream and green onions.

Holiday Helper

One-dish meals are ideal for the hustle and bustle of the holiday season. With an ovenproof pan, a plan, and a few cans you can create this Mexican spin on pot pie to feed a crowd in minimal time. Browning the meat with the aromatics and seasonings really brings out the flavors. Turn to your cast-iron skillet for best results from start to finish. If you care for cast iron correctly, you will find that it is the most versatile nonstick pan around for both stovetop and oven cooking. Follow these simple steps to keep yours in tip-top shape:

HOW TO CARE FOR CAST IRON:

- Rid cast iron of rust stains with a gritty rubber stain eraser made for rust removal that you can find at hardware stores, bike shops, or woodworking shops. Simply rub off the stain, and then re-season the pan.
- For everyday cleaning, use a stiff brush or plastic scrubber under running water while the cast iron is still warm but cool enough to handle with ease. Kosher salt is also a good scrubbing agent for baked-on stains. The most important tip is to never use soap!
- Before cooking, apply vegetable oil to the cooking surface, and preheat the pan on low heat, increasing the temperature slowly.
- Never marinate in cast iron. Acidic mixtures will damage the seasoning. Re-season if food particles start to stick, rust appears, or you experience a metallic taste.

Short Rib and Stout Pies

SERVES 6
HANDS-ON 1 HOUR TOTAL 4 HOURS, 50 MINUTES

Complex flavors make these mini pies unforgettable.

6	pounds large short ribs
1	tablespoon table salt
2	teaspoons black pepper
¼	cup all-purpose flour
2	tablespoons extra virgin olive oil
4	celery ribs, chopped (about ¾-inch pieces)
1	large onion, chopped (about ¾-inch pieces)
4	carrots, chopped (about ¾-inch pieces)
2	bay leaves (fresh or dried)
1	tablespoon chopped fresh thyme
1	tablespoon fresh rosemary leaves, chopped
½	teaspoon fennel seeds
¼	teaspoon crushed red pepper
2	large garlic cloves, minced
1	(12-ounce) bottle extra-stout ale
3	cups beef broth
3	tablespoons brandy
1	tablespoon balsamic vinegar
1	teaspoon sugar
2	puff pastry sheets, thawed
1	large egg, beaten

1. Season ribs with salt and pepper, and let stand at room temperature 30 minutes. Toss ribs in flour, and shake off excess (reserve excess flour).

2. Heat 2 tablespoons oil in a large, ovenproof Dutch oven over medium-high heat. Cook ribs, in batches, in hot oil until dark brown on all sides.

3. Preheat oven to 300°F. Drain oil from Dutch oven, reserving 1 tablespoon oil in Dutch oven. Reduce heat to medium. Add celery and next 8 ingredients, and cook, stirring occasionally, 10 minutes or until onion is translucent. Add reserved flour and any salt and pepper that was left after coating ribs; cook 30 seconds.

4. Add stout, stirring to loosen browned bits from bottom of Dutch oven. Add broth and next 3 ingredients, and return ribs to Dutch oven. Bring to a boil; cover with lid.

5. Bake at 300°F, covered, for 2 hours. Uncover and bake 1 hour or until ribs are very tender but retain their shape.

6. Remove ribs from stew, and cool slightly. Increase oven temperature to 400°F.

7. Cook liquid and vegetables in Dutch oven over medium-high heat until liquid is reduced to about 4 cups; remove fat from surface of liquid as it cooks.

8. When cool enough to handle, coarsely shred meat, discarding bones. Stir meat into stew, and season with salt to taste. Ladle stew into 6 (10- to 12-ounce) deep, ovenproof soup bowls or large ramekins.

9. Roll out puff pastry sheets on a flat surface; cut out 6 rounds about ½ inch larger than soup bowls. Arrange pastry rounds over soup.

10. Whisk together egg and 1 tablespoon water. Brush pastry with egg mixture. Arrange soup bowls on an aluminum foil-lined baking sheet.

11. Bake at 400°F for 15 to 20 minutes or until pastry is golden brown. Remove from oven, and cool 5 minutes.

Fresh Idea

Leftover puff pastry? Combine it with that beloved Southern pantry staple, pepper jelly, for an addictive holiday party nibble: sweet-and-savory palmiers (the French word for "palm tree"). Try this Pepper Jelly version or the Parmesan and Caramelized Shallot Palmiers (page 140).

PEPPER JELLY PALMIERS:

1	(17.3-ounce) package frozen puff pastry sheets, thawed
	Parchment paper
1	cup plus 2 tablespoons finely shredded Parmesan cheese
6	tablespoons chopped fresh chives
½	teaspoon kosher salt
½	teaspoon freshly ground black pepper
½	cup hot pepper jelly

1. Roll 1 pastry sheet into a 12- x 10-inch rectangle on lightly floured parchment paper. Sprinkle with half of cheese, 3 tablespoons chives, and ¼ teaspoon each of salt and pepper. Roll up pastry, jelly-roll fashion, starting with each short side and ending at middle of pastry sheet. Wrap pastry tightly with parchment paper. Repeat procedure with remaining pastry sheet, cheese, chives, and remaining salt and pepper. Freeze 1 to 24 hours.

2. Preheat oven to 375°F. Remove pastries from freezer, and let stand at room temperature 10 minutes. Cut each roll into ¼-inch-thick slices, and place on parchment paper-lined baking sheets.

3. Bake, in batches, at 375°F for 20 minutes or until golden.

4. Microwave pepper jelly in a microwave-safe bowl at HIGH 1 minute. Spread ½ teaspoon pepper jelly onto each palmier. Serve immediately.

Herb-Crusted Salmon

SERVES 4 TO 6
HANDS-ON 10 MINUTES TOTAL 30 MINUTES

Lots of herbs transform this salmon from special to extraordinary. Be sure that all of the pin bones are removed from the fish.

1   (2½-pound) salmon fillet, pin bones removed
Parchment paper
1½ cups panko (Japanese breadcrumbs)
¼   cup loosely packed fresh flat-leaf parsley leaves, chopped
¼   cup loosely packed fresh dill, chopped
¼   cup loosely packed fresh basil leaves, chopped
2   garlic cloves, finely minced
6   tablespoons unsalted butter, melted
2   tablespoons honey mustard
2   teaspoons fresh thyme leaves, chopped
2   teaspoons lemon zest
2   tablespoons fresh lemon juice
2   teaspoons kosher salt
1   teaspoon black pepper
Lemon wedges

1. Preheat oven to 425°F. Rinse salmon, and pat dry with paper towels. Place salmon, skin side down, on a parchment paper-lined baking sheet.

2. Stir together panko and next 11 ingredients in a bowl. Gently press mixture onto salmon to form a thick crust.

3. Bake at 425°F for 20 minutes or until salmon is just cooked through and flakes easily with a fork. Serve immediately with lemon wedges.

Squash Galette with Fontina and Caramelized Onions

SERVES 10
HANDS-ON 15 MINUTES TOTAL 2 HOURS, 25 MINUTES

Caramelizing onions and making fresh dough requires work, but it's worth it for this complex and delicious side.

2½ cups all-purpose flour
2   teaspoons table salt
½   teaspoon freshly ground black pepper
1   cup unsalted butter, chilled and cut into ½-inch cubes
¼   cup buttermilk
¼   cup ice-cold water
2   (1¼-pound) packages fresh cubed butternut squash
3   tablespoons olive oil
Parchment paper
1   tablespoon unsalted butter
2   pounds Vidalia onions, thinly sliced
1½ teaspoons fresh thyme leaves, chopped
¼   teaspoon sugar
1   (8-ounce) wedge fontina cheese, coarsely shredded
1   large egg, beaten

1. Pulse flour, ½ teaspoon of the salt, and ¼ teaspoon of the pepper in a food processor until blended. Add 1 cup cubed butter, and pulse until mixture is the texture of coarse sand. Add buttermilk and ice-cold water, and pulse just until a dough forms. Pat dough into a disk, wrap in plastic wrap, and chill at least 1 hour or up to 2 days.

2. Preheat oven to 400°F. Toss squash with 1 tablespoon of the oil, ½ teaspoon salt, and remaining ¼ teaspoon pepper. Spread in a single layer on a parchment paper-lined baking sheet.

3. Bake at 400°F for 30 minutes or until squash is tender, stirring once halfway through baking.

4. Meanwhile, melt 1 tablespoon butter with remaining 2 tablespoons oil in a heavy skillet over medium-low heat. Add onion, thyme, sugar, and remaining 1 teaspoon salt, and cook, stirring occasionally, 25 to 30 minutes or until onions are caramelized. Let cool.

5. Roll dough into a 16-inch circle on a flat surface. Transfer to a parchment paper-lined pizza pan or baking sheet. Spread half of onions onto dough, leaving a 2-inch border. Top with half of cheese. Top with squash and remaining onions and cheese. Fold border over filling, pleating as needed, leaving center open.

6. Whisk together egg and 2 tablespoons water. Brush outside of dough with egg mixture. Bake at 400°F for 40 to 50 minutes or until golden brown.

Ultimate Macaroni and Cheese

SERVES 10 TO 12
HANDS-ON 20 MINUTES TOTAL 40 MINUTES

It seems that everyone at the holiday meal loves mac and cheese. It's comfort food at its finest and is best when presented in a deep dish with a crispy, crunchy topping.

1   (16-ounce) box mini penne pasta
½   cup unsalted butter
½   cup all-purpose flour
1   quart milk
1   (8-ounce) block Havarti cheese, grated
1   (8-ounce) block sharp white Cheddar cheese, grated
1   (8-ounce) wedge Parmesan cheese, grated and divided
1   teaspoon table salt
½   teaspoon freshly ground black pepper
Dash of freshly ground nutmeg
Dash of ground red pepper
½   (12-ounce) day-old French bread baguette, slightly stale
¼   cup salted butter
¼   cup chopped fresh flat-leaf parsley

1. Preheat oven to 350°F. Prepare pasta according to package directions for al dente.

2. Melt ½ cup unsalted butter in a large saucepan over medium-high heat. Whisk in flour, and cook, whisking constantly, 1 to 2 minutes. Gradually whisk in milk until well blended. Reduce heat to medium, and cook, stirring often, 5 minutes or until sauce thickens enough to coat back of a spoon. Add Havarti cheese, Cheddar cheese, and half of the Parmesan cheese; stir well until smooth. Remove from heat, and stir in salt, pepper, nutmeg, and red pepper.

3. Add cheese sauce to pasta, and stir to coat. Spoon mixture into a lightly greased 13- x 9-inch baking dish.

4. Bake at 350°F for 10 minutes.

5. Meanwhile, pulse bread in a food processor until coarsely crumbled. Melt ¼ cup butter in a small microwave-safe bowl at HIGH 30 seconds or until melted. Add breadcrumbs, parsley, remaining Parmesan cheese, and salt and pepper to taste, tossing to coat breadcrumbs. Sprinkle breadcrumb mixture over top of pasta mixture.

6. Bake at 350°F for 10 to 15 minutes or until topping is crispy and golden brown.

Whole Roasted Cauliflower with Ricotta-Pecorino Crust

SERVES 6
HANDS-ON 30 MINUTES TOTAL 1 HOUR

Not only is this dish incredibly impressive on the table, but it can be poached a full day ahead, then roasted last minute after your guests have arrived. No worries.

1   (750-milliliter) bottle dry white wine
½   cup kosher salt
1   large Vidalia onion, cut into wedges
3   bay leaves, halved
3   garlic cloves, smashed
2   fresh thyme sprigs
1   tablespoon dried crushed red pepper
3   medium lemons, zested and juiced
2½   pounds fresh cauliflower, trimmed and
       outer leaves removed
Parchment paper
1   cup whole-milk ricotta cheese
¼   cup plain Greek yogurt
2   ounces Pecorino Romano cheese, shredded
1   tablespoon extra virgin olive oil
¼   cup panko (Japanese breadcrumbs)
1½   teaspoons chopped fresh parsley

1. Preheat oven to 400°F. Combine first 7 ingredients, lemon juice and lemons, and 1 gallon water in a very large saucepan, and bring to a boil. Reduce heat; simmer 5 minutes or until onions are soft. Remove solids using a slotted spoon.

2. Return liquid to a simmer, and add cauliflower; simmer 13 minutes or until a knife inserted into center of cauliflower is met with slight resistance. Carefully remove cauliflower from pan, and drain in a colander. Place on a parchment paper-lined jelly-roll pan.

3. Stir together ricotta, yogurt, cheese, oil, and 1 teaspoon lemon zest until smooth. Season with table salt and pepper to taste.

4. Combine panko, parsley, and ¼ teaspoon lemon zest. Coat outside of cauliflower with ricotta mixture. Coat with panko mixture.

5. Bake at 400°F for 20 minutes or until golden brown.

Caramel Apple Pie with Browned Butter Crust

SERVES 10
HANDS-ON 45 MINUTES TOTAL 8 HOURS, 15 MINUTES

Browning the butter for the crust provides an extra hint of nuttiness but is not essential. Feel free to use cold butter instead and skip Step 1. Make both the crust and caramel sauce up to 2 days in advance to save time.

CRUST:
- 1   cup unsalted butter
- 2½ cups all-purpose flour
- 2   tablespoons granulated sugar
- 1   teaspoon table salt
- ½   cup plus 1 tablespoon cold buttermilk

CARAMEL:
- 1   cup granulated sugar
- ½   cup salted butter, cut into pieces
- 1   cup heavy cream

FILLING:
- ½   cup firmly packed brown sugar
- 3   tablespoons cornstarch
- ½   teaspoon ground cinnamon
- ¼   teaspoon freshly grated nutmeg
- 2   pounds Granny Smith apples, peeled and cut into ¾-inch slices
- 2   pounds Honeycrisp apples, peeled and cut into ¾-inch slices
- 1   tablespoon fresh lemon juice
- 1   large egg, lightly beaten

1. Prepare Crust: Cook butter in a heavy saucepan over medium heat, stirring constantly, 7 minutes or until butter begins to turn golden brown. Remove pan immediately from heat, and pour butter into a small bowl. Cover and chill 3 hours or until butter is cold and solidified.

2. Pulse flour, sugar, and salt in a food processor until blended. Cut browned butter into small pieces; add to processor, and pulse until mixture resembles coarse meal. Gradually add ½ cup buttermilk, pulsing until dough is moistened and just begins to come together, adding an additional 1 tablespoon buttermilk, if needed. Turn dough out onto a flat surface; divide in half. Gently gather each half into a ball; press into a flat disk, and wrap in plastic wrap. Chill 1 hour or until firm.

3. Prepare Caramel: Combine sugar and ¼ cup water in a medium saucepan over medium-high heat. Bring to a boil, brushing sides of pan with a wet pastry brush to prevent crystals from forming. Cook 8 minutes or

until amber colored. Remove from heat; whisk in butter and cream (mixture will bubble vigorously). Cook over medium-low heat, whisking constantly, 2 to 3 minutes or until smooth.

4. Prepare Filling: Preheat oven to 350°F. Combine brown sugar and next 3 ingredients in a large bowl; add apples, lemon juice, and ½ cup caramel sauce, and toss until blended.

5. Roll each dough round into a 13-inch circle on a lightly floured surface. Fit one dough round into a 9½-inch deep-dish pie plate; spoon apple mixture into dish. Top with remaining dough round; seal edges, and crimp. Brush dough with egg. Cut several slits in dough to allow steam to escape.

6. Bake at 350°F for 1 hour and 30 minutes or until crust is deep golden brown, apples are tender, and filling is bubbly, shielding with aluminum foil if needed. (Place a baking sheet on the oven rack below the pie while baking.) Cool pie on a wire rack 2 hours. Serve with remaining caramel sauce.

Holiday Helper

September through November are peak apple harvest months. It's a great time to show them off in recipes.

How many apples do I buy? Two pounds of apples make a typical 9-inch pie. For each pound of apples called for in a recipe, you'll need to purchase either:

4 small apples
3 medium apples
2 large apples

1 pound = 3 cups diced or 2¾ cups sliced

Peel apples with a sharp paring knife or vegetable peeler. The tip of many vegetable peelers or special apple corers make removing the nonedible core a cinch. To keep cut apples from browning, dip in pineapple juice or a mixture of lemon juice and water.

Amaretti-Chocolate Tart

SERVES 8
HANDS-ON 15 MINUTES TOTAL 4 HOURS, 40 MINUTES

Crispy Italian amaretti cookies add lovely contrast to the creamy almond frangipane filling.

CRUST:
1¼ cups all-purpose flour
1½ tablespoons sugar
½ cup cold butter, cut into pieces
2 tablespoons ice-cold water
1 large egg yolk

FILLING:
1 (4-ounce) bittersweet chocolate baking bar, chopped
½ cup butter, softened
½ cup sugar
1 large egg
2 tablespoons brandy
1 teaspoon vanilla extract
1 cup finely ground blanched almonds (almond meal/flour)
1 tablespoon all-purpose flour
12 amaretti cookies, coarsely crushed (¾ cup)
⅓ cup sliced almonds

1. Prepare Crust: Combine flour and sugar in a medium bowl; cut in butter with a pastry blender until mixture resembles fine meal. Whisk water with egg yolk; gradually add to flour mixture, stirring with a fork until dry ingredients are moistened. Gather into a ball, shape into a disk, and wrap in plastic wrap. Chill 1 hour until firm.

2. Preheat oven to 375°F. Roll dough to a 12-inch round (about ⅛-inch thick) on a floured surface. Fit in a 9-inch tart pan with removable bottom; trim edges. Line dough with foil; fill with dried beans or pie weights.

3. Bake at 375°F for 15 minutes or until edges are lightly browned. Remove foil and pie weights; bake 10 minutes more. Cool on a wire rack (about 30 minutes).

4. Prepare Filling: Microwave chocolate in a small microwave-safe bowl at HIGH 1 to 1½ minutes until melted; stir at 30-second intervals. Cool 5 minutes.

5. Beat butter and sugar at medium speed with an electric mixer until light and fluffy; beat in egg, brandy, and vanilla until well blended. Beat in ground almonds and all-purpose flour at low speed until blended. Gradually add melted chocolate, beating at low speed just until blended. Spread mixture in an even layer in tart shell. Sprinkle with amaretti cookies and sliced almonds.

6. Bake at 375°F for 25 minutes or until puffed, lightly browned, and set. Cool completely on a wire rack (about 2 hours).

Cherry-Almond Crumb Cake

SERVES 10 TO 12
HANDS-ON 20 MINUTES TOTAL 1 HOUR, 25 MINUTES

Fragrant and sweet, this is destined to be a holiday classic.

STREUSEL:
½ cup all-purpose flour
½ cup firmly packed brown sugar
½ teaspoon ground cinnamon
¼ cup butter, cut into pieces
½ cup sliced almonds

CAKE:
1 (5-ounce) package dried tart cherries (about 1 cup)
2½ cups all-purpose flour
1 teaspoon baking powder
½ teaspoon baking soda
½ teaspoon ground cardamom
½ teaspoon ground cinnamon
¼ teaspoon table salt
¾ cup butter, softened
1¼ cups granulated sugar
3 large eggs
1 teaspoon vanilla extract
1¼ cups sour cream

GLAZE:
½ cup powdered sugar
¼ cup sour cream
¼ teaspoon vanilla extract

1. Prepare Streusel: Combine first 3 ingredients; cut in butter with a pastry blender until it resembles small peas. Stir in almonds. Cover and chill until ready to use.

2. Prepare Cake: Preheat oven to 350°F. Bring 2 cups water to a simmer in a small saucepan; add cherries. Remove from heat; let stand 5 minutes or until cherries soften. Drain.

3. Whisk 2½ cups flour with next 5 ingredients in a bowl. Toss cherries with 1 tablespoon flour mixture.

4. Beat ¾ cup butter at medium speed with an electric mixer until creamy. Add granulated sugar; beat until light and fluffy. Add eggs, 1 at a time; beating after each addition. Beat in vanilla. Add flour mixture to butter mixture alternately with sour cream. Beat at low speed just until blended after each addition. Fold in cherries. Spoon batter into a greased and floured 10-inch (12-cup) tube pan; sprinkle with streusel.

5. Bake at 350°F for 50 minutes or until a wooden pick inserted in center comes out clean. Cool in pan on rack 15 minutes; remove from pan to wire rack to cool completely.

6. Prepare Glaze: Combine all ingredients; drizzle over cake.

Rosemary-Blue Cheese Crackers

MAKES 8 DOZEN
HANDS-ON 15 MINUTES TOTAL 3 HOURS, 45 MINUTES

Give these crackers in glassine bags tied with string for a festive party gift.

16 ounces blue cheese, softened and crumbled
1   cup unsalted butter, softened
2   tablespoons finely chopped fresh rosemary
2   teaspoons kosher salt
1½ teaspoons freshly ground black pepper
3   cups all-purpose flour
Parchment paper

1. Beat first 5 ingredients with a heavy-duty electric stand mixer at medium speed, using paddle attachment, 2 to 3 minutes or until creamy and well blended. Gradually add flour, beating at low speed just until blended and dough comes together. Divide dough in half; roll each half into a 12-inch-long, 1½-inch-thick log. Wrap in plastic wrap, and chill until firm (at least 2 hours).

2. Preheat oven to 350°F. Cut logs into ¼-inch-thick slices using a sharp knife; place on parchment paper-lined baking sheets. (Work with one log at a time to ensure that slices remain chilled before baking.)

3. Bake at 350°F for 18 to 20 minutes or until edges are deep golden brown. Cool on baking sheets 5 minutes; transfer to wire racks, and cool completely (about 15 minutes; crackers will crisp as they cool).

NOTE: You can keep these logs on hand in your freezer for last-minute gifts and appetizer options. Let them stand at room temperature 15 minutes or until sliceable. For a decorative touch, press a couple of fresh rosemary leaves onto each cracker before baking.

Parmesan and Caramelized Shallot Palmiers

MAKES 2 DOZEN
HANDS-ON 30 MINUTES TOTAL 2 HOURS, 5 MINUTES

Double this recipe to use the entire box of puff pastry. These also make an excellent holiday appetizer.

2   tablespoons butter
1½ cups finely chopped shallots (about 7 medium shallots)
2   teaspoons chopped fresh thyme
½   teaspoon table salt
¼   teaspoon freshly ground black pepper
½   (17.3-ounce) package puff pastry sheets, thawed (1 sheet)
1   large egg, lightly beaten
1   cup grated Parmigiano-Reggiano cheese (about 4 ounces)
Parchment paper

1. Melt butter in a medium skillet over medium heat. Add shallots; cook, stirring often, 15 minutes or until caramelized. Remove from heat, and stir in thyme, salt, and pepper. Cool 10 minutes.

2. Unroll pastry on a lightly floured surface; brush lightly with egg. Spread shallot mixture over pastry, and sprinkle with cheese. Roll in two opposite sides, jelly-roll fashion, to meet in center. Brush beaten egg between rolled sides; press lightly to seal. Wrap in plastic wrap, and freeze 45 minutes or until well chilled and almost firm.

3. Preheat oven to 400°F. Cut pastry into 24 slices (about ⅜-inch thick) using a sharp knife; place on a parchment paper-lined baking sheet. Brush lightly with egg.

4. Bake at 400°F for 18 to 20 minutes or until golden brown. Cool on baking sheet 5 minutes; transfer to wire rack, and cool completely (15 minutes).

Savory Herbed Biscotti

MAKES ABOUT 3 DOZEN
HANDS-ON 30 MINUTES TOTAL 2 HOURS, 30 MINUTES

*This delightful take on a simple crostini will complement
your aperitifs during the cocktail hour. As these are not
meant to be dipped in a liquid, they are more tender than
you might expect from biscotti. Serve with your favorite
Camembert or other soft-ripened cheese. Be sure to use
fresh dates, not pre-chopped, for the best results.*

4	cups all-purpose flour
2	tablespoons finely chopped fresh flat-leaf parsley
1	tablespoon baking powder
2	teaspoons finely chopped fresh rosemary
1½	teaspoons kosher salt
½	cup chopped pitted dates (about 6 Medjool dates)
1	cup unsalted butter, softened
4	ounces goat cheese, softened
3	tablespoons sugar
3	tablespoons honey
4	large eggs, at room temperature

Parchment paper

1. Preheat oven to 350°F. Whisk together first
5 ingredients in a medium bowl. Stir in dates.

2. Beat butter and goat cheese at medium speed with
a heavy-duty electric stand mixer until smooth, using
the paddle attachment. Add sugar and honey; beat
at medium speed until well blended. Add eggs, one at
a time, beating well after each addition. Gradually
add flour mixture, beating at medium-low speed until
just blended.

3. Divide dough in half. Shape each portion into
2 (14- x 2-inch) slightly flattened logs on a parchment
paper-lined baking sheet, using slightly dampened
hands.

4. Bake at 350°F for 30 minutes or until light golden
brown and logs resist slightly when touched. Cool
on baking sheets on a wire rack 30 minutes.

5. Reduce oven temperature to 300°F. Cut each log
diagonally into ½-inch-thick slices with a serrated knife,
using a gentle sawing motion. Place slices on ungreased
baking sheets.

6. Bake at 300°F for 15 minutes; turn over, and bake
15 minutes or until golden brown. Transfer to wire
racks, and cool completely (about 30 minutes).

Homemade All-Purpose Biscuit, Pancake, and Waffle Mix

MAKES ABOUT 8 CUPS
HANDS-ON 5 MINUTES TOTAL 5 MINUTES

This mix can be used to make flaky buttermilk biscuits, fluffy pancakes, and your new favorite waffles. Your friends will thank you—that is, if you can muster parting with this batch.

6	cups all-purpose flour
1½	cups powdered buttermilk
¼	cup granulated sugar
2	tablespoons baking powder
1	tablespoon baking soda
1½	teaspoons salt

Whisk together all ingredients in a large bowl. Store in airtight containers up to 6 months.

NOTE: We tested with Saco Cultured Buttermilk Powder.

Time-Saver

When making a batch of this mix to give, be sure to include recipe cards with the instructions for how to make the pancakes, biscuits, and waffles, but also make a batch or two for your kitchen. It makes getting a from-scratch breakfast on the table no problem during this busy time of year.

Homemade Biscuits

MAKES 6 (2½-INCH) BISCUITS
HANDS-ON 20 MINUTES TOTAL 35 MINUTES

These light, fluffy biscuits are tailor-made for slathering with butter or smothering with sausage cream gravy.

Preheat oven to 450°F. Cut 5 tablespoons cold butter, cut into cubes, into 2⅔ cups Homemade All-Purpose Biscuit, Pancake, and Waffle Mix using a pastry blender. Add ½ to ¾ cup ice-cold water, ¼ cup at a time, stirring with a wooden spoon after each addition (dough will be shaggy and sticky). Turn dough out onto a lightly floured surface, and knead 3 or 4 times; pat into a ¾-inch-thick rectangle. Cut dough into rounds, using a 2½-inch round cutter. Place on a parchment paper-lined baking sheet, and bake at 450°F for 15 minutes or until golden brown.

Homemade Pancakes

MAKES 18 (4-INCH) PANCAKES
HANDS-ON 20 MINUTES TOTAL 25 MINUTES

Add a twist to your pancakes by whisking in ½ teaspoon extract with the water, 1 cup berries, or ½ cup chopped nuts after whisking the mix into the wet ingredients.

Whisk together 1½ cups water, 2 large eggs, and 3 tablespoons canola or vegetable oil (or melted butter). Gently whisk in 2⅔ cups Homemade All-Purpose Biscuit, Pancake, and Waffle Mix just until blended (do not overmix), and let stand 5 minutes. Pour about ¼ cup batter for each pancake onto a hot, lightly greased griddle or large nonstick skillet. Cook pancakes over medium heat 1 to 2 minutes or until tops are covered with bubbles and edges look dry and cooked; turn and cook other side. Serve with maple syrup.

Homemade Waffles

MAKES 12 (4-INCH) BELGIAN WAFFLES
HANDS-ON 20 MINUTES TOTAL 25 MINUTES

Crisp outside, tender inside, waffles topped with syrup or whipped cream and berries make mornings great.

Whisk 1½ cups water and ½ cup vegetable oil (or melted butter) with 2 large egg yolks. Beat 2 large egg whites at high speed with an electric mixer until stiff (2 minutes). Gently whisk 2⅔ cups Homemade All-Purpose Biscuit, Pancake, and Waffle Mix into oil mixture, and fold in beaten egg whites. Coat a preheated waffle iron with cooking spray; add ½ cup batter to waffle iron. Cook 2 to 3 minutes or until golden. Serve with maple syrup.

Mustard-Dill Sauce

MAKES 6 CUPS
HANDS-ON 10 MINUTES TOTAL 10 MINUTES

*Use this sauce as a base/starter for vinaigrettes, sauces,
or marinades, or use it on its own with gravlax and
toasted rye bread as a quick appetizer.*

Stir together 3 cups Dijon mustard, 1½ cups chopped
fresh dill (about 2 [1-ounce] packages), 1 cup honey,
½ cup extra virgin olive oil, ½ cup white wine vinegar,
and 2 tablespoons dry white wine. Divide sauce among
small jars, and label.

Smoky Porcini Salt

MAKES 1¾ CUPS
HANDS-ON 15 MINUTES TOTAL 15 MINUTES

This salt will add a slight smoky umami flavor to foods. It's perfect on steak, chicken, and buttered bread.

- ½ cup hickory wood chips
- 1 (8.5-ounce) box flaky sea salt
- 1 (1-ounce) package dried porcini mushrooms

1. Pierce 10 holes in bottom of a 13- x 9-inch disposable aluminum pan. Arrange wood chips over holes. Place salt on opposite side of pan.

2. Place pan on stovetop burner with holes over burner; heat burner to medium until wood chips begin to smoke. Reduce heat to medium-low; cover pan with aluminum foil, and seal tightly. Cook 4 minutes or until salt is a light tan color and tastes smoky. Remove from heat, and transfer salt to a bowl.

3. Grind mushrooms into a fine powder in a spice grinder (about ⅓ cup). Combine porcini powder and smoked salt, and transfer to small jars.

Garlic-and-Herb-Infused Oil

MAKES ABOUT 3 CUPS
HANDS-ON 10 MINUTES TOTAL 4 HOURS, 10 MINUTES

Be sure to thoroughly wash and dry the herbs before adding to the oil to prevent bacterial growth.

- 3 cups extra virgin olive oil
- 5 garlic cloves, smashed
- 3 fresh thyme sprigs
- 3 fresh rosemary sprigs
- 3 fresh sage sprigs
- 2 bay leaves
- 1 teaspoon fennel seeds
- 1 teaspoon coriander seeds
- 1 teaspoon crushed red pepper

Cheesecloth

1. Cook first 9 ingredients in a large, deep skillet over medium heat 5 minutes or until oil warms and garlic and herbs begin to sizzle.

2. Remove from heat, and cool completely (about 4 hours).

3. Pour oil through a cheesecloth-lined strainer into a bowl; discard solids. Transfer infused oil into small bottles, and label. Store in refrigerator up to 1 month.

Homemade Bourbon "Irish" Crème

MAKES 4 CUPS
HANDS-ON 5 MINUTES TOTAL 5 MINUTES

You'll wow your friends with this fun party gift. Use as you would Bailey's Irish Cream.

- 1⅔ cups bourbon
- 1 (14-ounce) can sweetened condensed milk
- 1 cup heavy cream
- 2 tablespoons chocolate syrup
- 1 teaspoon instant coffee
- 2 teaspoons vanilla extract

Process all ingredients in a blender until smooth. Pour into individual gift jars. Store in refrigerator up to 2 weeks.

Bonus

50
Years of Sweets

Bourbon balls, bonbons, caramels, and clusters, since 1966 more sweet treats have come from the Southern Living Test Kitchen than we can count. Enjoy fifty favorites.

Brown Sugar-Cocoa Fudge *(1966)*

**MAKES 3 DOZEN
HANDS-ON 20 MIN.
TOTAL 1 HR., 20 MIN.**

Parchment paper
2   cups packed light brown sugar
2   cups granulated sugar
1   cup milk
6   Tbsp. unsweetened cocoa
3   Tbsp. light corn syrup
¼   tsp. cream of tartar
⅛   tsp. table salt
3   Tbsp. butter
2   tsp. vanilla extract

1. Line bottom and sides of a 9-inch square pan with parchment paper, allowing 2 to 3 inches to extend over sides.

2. Combine brown sugar and next 6 ingredients in a heavy 4-qt. saucepan. Bring to a boil over medium-high heat; cook 4 minutes, stirring constantly, or until a candy thermometer registers 240°F (soft ball stage). Remove from heat; stir in butter and vanilla. Beat 3 to 4 minutes with a wooden spoon or until mixture begins to thicken. Pour into prepared pan, spreading evenly. Cool completely (about 1 hour). Lift out of pan using parchment as handles; cut into 1½-inch squares.

Mexican Pecan Candy *(1966)*

**MAKES 2 DOZEN PIECES
HANDS-ON 21 MIN.
TOTAL 1 HR., 21 MIN.**

Parchment paper
2   cups sugar
1   cup milk
2   Tbsp. butter
2   Tbsp. light corn syrup
½   tsp. table salt
¼   tsp. baking soda
1   cup chopped pecans
1   tsp. vanilla extract

1. Line bottom and sides of an 8-inch square pan with parchment paper, allowing 2 to 3 inches to extend over sides.

2. Combine sugar and next 5 ingredients in a large saucepan; bring to a boil over medium-high heat. Stir in pecans; cook 8 minutes, stirring constantly, or until a candy thermometer registers 234°F (soft ball stage). Remove from heat; stir in vanilla. Beat 3 to 4 minutes with a wooden spoon or until creamy and beginning to thicken. Pour into pan, spreading evenly. Cool completely (about 1 hour). Lift out of pan using parchment as handles; cut into small rectangles.

Leche Quemada *(1968)*

**MAKES 2 DOZEN PIECES
HANDS-ON 20 MIN. TOTAL 20 MIN.**

1   (5-oz.) can evaporated milk
3   cups sugar
3   Tbsp. butter
2   Tbsp. light corn syrup
2   cups coarsely chopped pecans
Parchment paper

1. Pour evaporated milk into measuring cup; add water to make 1 cup. Place milk mixture, 2½ cups of the sugar, 2 Tbsp. of the butter, and corn syrup in a 4-qt. heavy saucepan. Bring to a boil over medium-high heat; stir in remaining ½ cup sugar, 1 Tbsp. butter, and pecans. Cook 8 minutes, stirring frequently, until a candy thermometer registers 240°F (soft ball stage).

2. Remove from heat; beat 3 to 4 minutes with a wooden spoon until creamy and slightly thickened. Quickly drop by spoonfuls onto parchment paper-lined baking sheets.

Ripple Divinity *(1968)*

**MAKES 4 DOZEN
HANDS-ON 20 MIN. TOTAL 20 MIN.**

3   cups sugar
½   cup light corn syrup
2   large egg whites
1   tsp. vanilla extract
1   cup semisweet chocolate morsels
Parchment paper

1. Combine sugar, corn syrup, and ½ cup water in a 2-qt. saucepan. Bring to a boil over medium-high heat; reduce heat to medium and cook 3 minutes or until a candy thermometer registers 240°F (soft ball stage).

2. Meanwhile, place egg whites in the bowl of a heavy-duty stand mixer. Beat at medium-high speed until soft peaks form. Slowly pour one-third of hot sugar mixture into egg whites in a thin stream, beating at medium-high speed. Reduce mixer speed to low.

3. Return sugar mixture to medium heat; cook 3 minutes or until a candy thermometer registers 265°F. Increase mixer speed to medium-high; slowly pour remaining sugar mixture into egg whites in a thin stream. Beat 7 minutes or until mixture just begins to hold its shape (do not overbeat; mixture will become more firm as it cools). Beat in vanilla.

4. Fold in chocolate morsels. (Since the mixture is warm, the chocolate pieces will partially melt and give a rippled appearance to the divinity.) Quickly drop by tablespoonfuls onto parchment paper-lined baking sheets.

Chocolate Balls *(1969)*

MAKES 9 DOZEN
HANDS-ON 30 MIN. TOTAL 1 HR.

1½ cups graham cracker crumbs
    (11 sheets)
1⅓ cups crunchy peanut butter
1   cup butter, melted
1   cup unsweetened shredded
    coconut
½   cup chopped toasted pecans
2   tsp. vanilla extract
1   (16-oz.) package powdered sugar
Parchment paper
2   (12-oz.) packages semisweet
    chocolate morsels
¼   cup shortening

1. Stir together first 7 ingredients until well blended. Roll mixture into 1-inch balls; place on parchment paper-lined baking sheets.

2. Microwave chocolate and shortening in a medium microwave-safe bowl 1 to 2 minutes, stirring every 30 seconds, or until melted and smooth. Using 2 forks, dip each ball into chocolate mixture, tapping off excess. Return to baking sheets. Let stand until set, or chill 30 minutes for a firmer coating.

1970S

Orange Candy *(1970)*

MAKES 40 PIECES
HANDS-ON 45 MIN.
TOTAL 2 HR., 5 MIN.

3   cups sugar
2   cups half-and-half
2   cups roasted salted pistachios
2   Tbsp. orange zest
Parchment paper

1. Combine sugar and half-and-half in a heavy 4-qt. saucepan; bring to a boil over medium-high heat. Reduce heat to medium and cook 20 minutes, stirring frequently, until a candy thermometer registers 240°F (soft ball stage). Remove from heat; cool 5 minutes.

2. Stir in pistachios and orange zest; beat with a wooden spoon 10 minutes or until mixture is almost stiff. Drop by tablespoonfuls onto parchment paper-lined baking sheets. Let stand 15 minutes; chill 1 hour or until firm. Store in an airtight container in refrigerator.

Orange Caramel Fudge *(1971)*

Most any nut could be substituted here—pistachios, hazelnuts, walnuts, almonds. Use what you love.

MAKES 42 PIECES
HANDS-ON 45 MIN.
TOTAL 1 HR., 45 MIN.

Parchment paper
3   cups sugar
1   cup evaporated milk
¼   tsp. salt

4   Tbsp. butter
2   tsp. orange zest
1   cup chopped toasted pecans

1. Line bottom and sides of an 8-inch square pan with parchment paper, allowing 2 to 3 inches to extend over sides.

2. Place 1 cup of the sugar in a heavy 3-qt. saucepan. Cook over medium heat 8 minutes or until sugar has caramelized, shaking pan frequently (do not stir). Carefully add ½ cup water and milk to sugar (mixture will bubble vigorously); cook over medium heat, stirring constantly, until caramel is dissolved.

3. Add remaining 2 cups sugar and salt; bring to a boil over medium heat. Reduce heat to low, and cook, stirring occasionally, 30 minutes or until a candy thermometer registers 242°F (firm ball stage). Remove from heat; add butter, zest, and pecans, stirring until butter is melted. Beat with a wooden spoon 3 to 5 minutes or until mixture thickens. Pour into pan, spreading evenly. Cool completely (about 1 hour). Lift out of pan using parchment as handles; cut into small pieces.

Chocolate Truffles *(1974)*

MAKES 2 DOZEN
HANDS-ON 15 MIN.
TOTAL 3 HR., 15 MIN.

3   oz. unsweetened chocolate
    baking bar, chopped
1¼ cups powdered sugar
⅓   cup butter, softened
2   Tbsp. light corn syrup
½   tsp. vanilla extract
¾   cup chopped toasted hazelnuts

1. Microwave chocolate in a microwave-safe bowl at HIGH

1 minute or until melted, stirring after 30 seconds.

2. Beat powdered sugar and butter at medium speed with an electric mixer until smooth. Beat in corn syrup and vanilla. Stir in chocolate. Place plastic wrap on surface of mixture; chill 3 hours or until firm.

3. Shape mixture into 1-inch balls with a small cookie scoop; roll in hazelnuts. Store in an airtight container in a cool place.

Divine Divinity *(1976)*

MAKES 3 DOZEN
HANDS-ON 20 MIN. TOTAL 20 MIN.

2½ cups sugar
½   cup light corn syrup
2   large egg whites
2   tsp. vanilla extract
1   cup chopped toasted pecans
Parchment paper

1. Combine sugar, corn syrup, and ½ cup water in a 2-qt. saucepan. Bring to a boil over medium-high heat; reduce heat to medium and cook 3 minutes or until a candy thermometer registers 234°F (thread stage).

2. Meanwhile, place egg whites in the bowl of a heavy-duty stand mixer. Beat at medium-high speed until soft peaks form. Slowly pour half of hot sugar mixture into egg whites in a thin stream, beating at medium-high speed. Reduce mixer speed to low.

3. Return sugar mixture to medium heat; cook 3 minutes or until a candy thermometer registers 265°F (hard ball stage). Increase mixer speed to medium-high; slowly pour remaining sugar mixture into egg whites in a thin stream. Beat 7 minutes or until mixture just begins to hold its shape (do not

overbeat; mixture will become more firm as it cools). Beat in vanilla.

4. Fold in pecans. Quickly drop by tablespoonfuls onto parchment paper-lined baking sheets.

Citrus Bonbons *(1977)*

MAKES 4 DOZEN
HANDS-ON 20 MIN.
TOTAL 1 HR., 20 MIN.

1   (11-oz.) box vanilla wafers, finely crushed (3 cups)
1   cup powdered sugar
1   cup finely chopped toasted pecans
¼   cup fresh lemon juice
¼   cup fresh orange juice
1   Tbsp. orange zest
½   cup granulated sugar
Parchment paper

Combine first 6 ingredients in a large bowl; mix well. Shape into 1-inch balls; roll in granulated sugar. Place on parchment paper-lined baking sheets, and let stand 1 hour. Store in an airtight container.

Coconut Caramels *(1977)*

MAKES 32 (1-INCH) PIECES
HANDS-ON 40 MIN.
TOTAL 2 HR., 40 MIN.

1   cup sugar
¾   cup light corn syrup
1½ cups half-and-half
1   cup sweetened flaked coconut
2   Tbsp. butter
1   tsp. vanilla extract
Parchment paper

1. Combine sugar, corn syrup, and ½ cup of the half-and-half in a heavy 3-qt. saucepan. Bring to

a boil over medium heat, stirring frequently. Reduce heat to medium-low, and cook 8 to 10 minutes, stirring constantly, until a candy thermometer registers 234°F (soft ball stage).

2. Stir in ½ cup half-and-half; cook 8 to 10 minutes, stirring constantly, until a candy thermometer registers 234°F. Stir in remaining ½ cup half-and-half; cook 8 to 10 minutes, stirring constantly, until a candy thermometer registers 234°F. Remove from heat; add coconut, butter, and vanilla. Stir until butter is melted.

3. Pour into an 8- x 4-inch loaf pan lined with parchment paper; let stand 2 hours or until firm. Lift candy out onto a cutting board. Cut into 1-inch squares using a sharp greased knife. Wrap individually in parchment paper or wax paper.

Kentucky Colonels *(1979)*

MAKES 6 DOZEN
HANDS-ON 30 MIN.
TOTAL 1 HR., 30 MIN.

½   cup butter, softened
6   Tbsp. bourbon
3   Tbsp. sweetened condensed milk
7½ cups powdered sugar
½   cup finely chopped toasted pecans
Parchment paper
2   (12-oz.) packages semisweet chocolate morsels
¼   cup shortening
Toasted pecan halves

1. Beat butter, bourbon, and condensed milk with a heavy-duty electric stand mixer fitted with the paddle attachment until blended (mixture may not be smooth). Gradually add powdered sugar, beating on low speed until blended and smooth. Beat in chopped pecans. Shape mixture into 1-inch balls; place on parchment paper-lined baking sheets. Chill 30 minutes or until firm.

2. Microwave chocolate morsels and shortening in a medium microwave-safe bowl at HIGH 1½ to 2 minutes or until melted, stirring every 30 seconds. Remove several balls from refrigerator at a time. Using a toothpick, dip each ball into chocolate mixture, tapping off excess. Place on parchment paper-lined baking sheets. Remove toothpick, and gently press a pecan half on each. Chill 30 minutes or until firm. Store in an airtight container in a cool place or in refrigerator.

NOTE: You will need 6 dozen pecan halves for this recipe

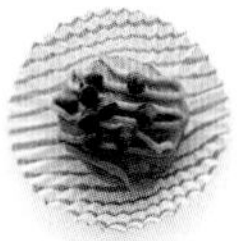

Peanut Butter Creams *(1979)*

MAKES 5 DOZEN
HANDS-ON 20 MIN. TOTAL 20 MIN.

1	cup creamy peanut butter
¾	cup sweetened condensed milk
¼	cup powdered sugar
½	cup semisweet chocolate mini-morsels
½	cup chocolate candy sprinkles

Combine peanut butter, condensed milk, and powdered sugar in a medium bowl; stir until well blended. Stir in chocolate mini-morsels. Shape into ¾-inch balls; roll in candy sprinkles. Store in an airtight container.

Chocolate Rum Balls *(1980)*

MAKES 5 DOZEN
HANDS-ON 30 MIN. TOTAL 1 HR.

1	cup semisweet chocolate morsels
1	Tbsp. dark rum
1	(7-oz.) jar marshmallow crème
3	cups crisp rice cereal
½	cup shredded unsweetened coconut
½	cup chopped toasted pecans
¼	cup unsweetened cocoa
¼	cup instant espresso powder

1. Microwave chocolate morsels and rum in a medium microwave-safe bowl at MEDIUM 1½ minutes, stirring every 30 seconds. Immediately stir in marshmallow crème. Stir in cereal, coconut, and pecans. Let stand at room temperature 30 minutes.

2. Combine cocoa and espresso powder in a small bowl. Shape mixture into 1-inch balls; roll in cocoa mixture.

Bourbon Balls *(1981)*

MAKES 5 DOZEN
HANDS-ON 25 MIN. TOTAL 25 MIN.

60	vanilla wafers, finely crushed (2 cups)
2	cups chopped toasted walnuts
2	cups powdered sugar
¼	cup unsweetened cocoa
6	Tbsp. bourbon
3	Tbsp. light corn syrup
	Powdered sugar

Combine first 4 ingredients in a large bowl; mix well. Combine

bourbon and corn syrup; add to crumb mixture, stirring until well blended. Shape into 1-inch balls; roll in powdered sugar. Store in an airtight container.

Nut Clusters *(1981)*

MAKES 2 DOZEN
HANDS-ON 15 MIN. TOTAL 45 MIN.

½	cup sugar
½	cup evaporated milk
1	Tbsp. light corn syrup
1	cup semisweet chocolate morsels
¾	cup roasted salted peanuts
	Parchment paper

1. Combine first 3 ingredients in a heavy 2-qt. saucepan; Bring to a boil over medium-high heat. Reduce heat to medium and cook, stirring constantly, until a candy thermometer registers 234°F (soft ball stage).

2. Remove from heat; add chocolate morsels, stirring until chocolate melts. Stir in peanuts. Drop by rounded teaspoonfuls onto parchment paper-lined baking sheets. Chill 30 minutes or until set.

NOTE: Coarsely chopped toasted pecans can be substituted for peanuts, if desired.

Peanut Butter Chocolate Candy Squares *(1982)*

MAKES 4 DOZEN
HANDS-ON 10 MIN. TOTAL 40 MIN.

1	cup butter, melted
1½	cups graham cracker crumbs (11 sheets)

1   cup peanut butter
1   (16-oz.) package powdered sugar
1   (12-oz.) package semisweet
    chocolate morsels

1. Line bottom and sides of a 13- x 9-inch pan with aluminum foil, allowing 2 to 3 inches to extend over sides.

2. Stir together first 4 ingredients until well blended. Press mixture evenly into pan.

3. Microwave chocolate in a medium microwave-safe bowl at HIGH 1 minute or until melted, stirring after 30 seconds. Spread melted chocolate evenly over mixture in pan. Chill 30 minutes. Lift out of pan using foil as handles; cut into 1½-inch squares.

Almond Truffles
(1983)

MAKES 2 DOZEN
HANDS-ON 15 MIN.
TOTAL 1 HR., 5 MIN.

3   Tbsp. butter, softened
½   cup powdered sugar
6   oz. semisweet chocolate
    baking bar, finely grated
2   Tbsp. white crème de cacao
24 whole natural almonds, toasted
½   cup finely chopped toasted
    whole natural almonds

1. Beat butter with an electric mixer on medium speed until smooth; add sugar and beat until blended. Beat in chocolate and crème de cacao. Cover and chill 1 hour.

2. Shape mixture into 1-inch balls, inserting one whole almond into center of each; roll in chopped almonds. Cover and chill 30 minutes. Store in an airtight container in refrigerator.

Pecan-Shortbread Sugarplums *(1983)*

MAKES 6 DOZEN
HANDS-ON 30 MIN.
TOTAL 3 HR., 55 MIN.

½   cup butter, softened
1   cup powdered sugar
3   Tbsp. brandy
2   Tbsp. light corn syrup
2½ cups Shortbread Cookie Crumbs
1   cup raisins
1   cup finely chopped pecans
¾   cup chopped dried pineapple
½   cup chopped red candied cherries
¼   cup finely chopped mixed
    candied fruit
1   (8-oz.) package pitted dates,
    chopped

Beat butter with an electric mixer at medium speed until creamy; gradually add powdered sugar, beating until light and fluffy. Beat in brandy and corn syrup. Stir in remaining ingredients. Shape mixture into 1-inch balls; roll in pecans, if desired. Chill 30 minutes or until firm. Store in an airtight container in refrigerator.

NOTE: These could be coated in chopped, toasted nuts, or toasted red velvet cake crumbs for interest.

Shortbread Cookie Crumbs

⅔   cup butter, softened
⅓   cup sugar
1½ cups all-purpose flour
Parchment paper

1. Beat butter with an electric mixer on medium speed until creamy; gradually add sugar, beating well. Beat in flour on low speed until just blended. Shape dough into an 8- x 2-inch log; wrap in plastic wrap. Chill 2 hours or until firm.

2. Preheat oven to 325°F. Cut log into ¼-inch-thick slices; place on parchment paper-lined baking sheets. Bake at 325°F for 20 minutes or until edges are golden brown. Cool completely on a wire rack (about 20 minutes). Crush cookies to yield about 2½ cups crumbs.

Peanut Butter Temptations *(1984)*

MAKES ABOUT 4 DOZEN
HANDS-ON 15 MIN.
TOTAL 2 HR., 10 MIN.

½   cup butter, softened
½   cup creamy peanut butter
½   cup granulated sugar
½   cup firmly packed brown sugar
1   large egg
½   tsp. vanilla extract
1¼ cups all-purpose flour
¾   tsp. baking soda
½   tsp. table salt
48 miniature peanut butter cup
    candies

1. Beat butter and peanut butter with an electric mixer at medium speed until creamy; gradually add sugars, beating until light and fluffy. Beat in egg and vanilla. Combine flour, baking soda, and salt; gradually add to butter mixture, beating on low speed until blended. Cover and chill dough 1 hour.

2. Preheat oven to 350°F. Shape dough into 48 (1-inch) balls; place in lightly greased miniature muffin pans, shaping each into a shell. Bake at 350°F for 12 minutes (dough will rise during baking). Remove from oven, and immediately press a miniature peanut butter cup into each hot crust. Cool in pan 20 minutes. Run knife or offset spatula around edge of each cup; carefully remove cookie. Cool completely on a wire rack (about 20 minutes).

Spiced Praline Delights *(1984)*

MAKES 2½ DOZEN
HANDS-ON 18 MIN.
TOTAL 38 MIN.

1   cup evaporated milk
1   (16-oz.) package light brown sugar
¼   cup butter
12   large marshmallows
1   tsp. ground cinnamon
¼   tsp. ground nutmeg
2   cups coarsely chopped toasted pecans
Parchment paper

1. Combine milk and sugar in a 4-qt. saucepan; bring to a boil over medium-high heat, stirring constantly. Reduce heat to medium and cook 7 minutes, stirring constantly, or until a candy thermometer registers 234°F (soft ball stage).

2. Remove from heat; stir in butter, marshmallows, cinnamon, and nutmeg until melted. Stir in pecans. Beat with a wooden spoon 3 to 5 minutes or until mixture is creamy and begins to thicken. Quickly drop mixture by rounded tablespoonfuls onto parchment paper-lined baking sheets; cool completely (about 20 minutes).

Caramel Peanut Squares *(1985)*

MAKES 3 DOZEN
HANDS-ON 20 MIN.
TOTAL 9 HR.

1   (12-oz.) package semisweet chocolate morsels
2   Tbsp. shortening

1   (14-oz.) package caramels
⅓   cup butter
1   cup coarsely chopped salted peanuts

1. Line bottom and sides of an 8-inch square pan with aluminum foil, allowing 2 to 3 inches to extend over sides. Lightly grease foil.

2. Microwave chocolate morsels and shortening in a medium microwave-safe bowl 1 to 1½ minutes, stirring every 30 seconds, until melted. Pour half of chocolate mixture into pan, spreading to edges in an even layer. Chill mixture in pan 15 minutes or until firm.

3. Combine caramels and butter in a heavy 2-qt. saucepan over low heat; cook, stirring frequently, until caramels melt. Stir in peanuts. Spoon mixture evenly over chocolate layer, spreading evenly. Chill 15 minutes or until cool.

4. Reheat remaining chocolate mixture in microwave, if necessary; pour evenly over caramel filling. Cover and chill 8 hours. Lift out of pan using foil as handles; let stand at room temperature 10 minutes. Cut into small squares.

Amaretto Dessert Truffles *(1986)*

MAKES 3½ DOZEN
HANDS-ON 25 MIN.
TOTAL 4 HR., 25 MIN.

12   oz. semisweet chocolate baking bar, chopped
½   cup butter, cut into pieces
2   large egg yolks
½   cup heavy whipping cream
⅓   cup amaretto liqueur
¾   cup finely chopped toasted sliced almonds

1. Combine chocolate and butter in a heat-proof bowl; place over simmering water and heat 1 to 2 minutes or until melted and smooth, stirring frequently.

2. Beat egg yolks with an electric mixer until thick and lemon colored. Gradually stir about one-fourth of warm chocolate mixture into yolks; gradually add to remaining chocolate mixture, stirring constantly. Stir in whipping cream and amaretto.

3. Place bowl over simmering water, and cook 2 to 3 minutes or until a thermometer registers 160°F, stirring constantly. (If mixture separates, whisk until smooth and emulsified.)

4. Cover and chill at least 4 hours or until firm. Use a small scoop to roll mixture into 1-inch balls; roll in almonds to coat. Store in an airtight container in refrigerator.

Plantation Coffee Pralines *(1986)*

MAKES 2 DOZEN
HANDS-ON 15 MIN.
TOTAL 45 MIN.

2   cups sugar
1   cup buttermilk
1   Tbsp. instant coffee powder
1   tsp. baking soda
⅛   tsp. salt
2   cups chopped toasted pecans
2   Tbsp. butter
2   tsp. vanilla extract
Parchment paper

1. Combine first 5 ingredients and ¼ cup water in a large Dutch oven; bring to a boil over medium heat, stirring constantly. Cook over medium heat, stirring constantly, until a candy thermometer registers 236°F (soft ball stage).

2. Remove from heat, and stir in pecans, butter, and vanilla. Beat with a wooden spoon 3 to 4 minutes until mixture just begins to thicken. Working rapidly, drop by rounded tablespoonfuls onto parchment paper-lined baking sheets. Cool completely (about 30 minutes).

White Chocolate Truffles *(1987)*

MAKES 2 DOZEN
HANDS-ON 15 MIN.
TOTAL 2 HR., 45 MIN.

- 8 oz. high quality white chocolate baking bar, coarsely chopped
- ⅓ cup butter
- ¾ cup finely chopped toasted blanched almonds

1. Microwave chocolate and butter in a microwave-safe bowl 1 minute, stirring every 15 seconds or just until melted and smooth (don't over-stir or mixture will separate). Place plastic wrap directly on surface of mixture; let stand at room temperature 2 hours or until firm.

2. Shape mixture into 1-inch balls; roll in almonds. Cover and chill 30 minutes. Store in an airtight container in refrigerator.

1990S

Almond Cream Confections *(1990)*

MAKES 3 DOZEN
HANDS-ON 25 MIN.
TOTAL 2 HR., 45 MIN.

- ½ cup butter
- ¼ cup sugar

- 2 Tbsp. unsweetened cocoa
- 2 tsp. vanilla extract
- ¼ tsp. table salt
- 1 large egg, lightly beaten
- 50 vanilla wafers, crushed (1¾ cups)
- 1 cup slivered almonds, toasted and chopped
- ½ cup sweetened flaked coconut
- Cream Filling
- Parchment paper
- 2 oz. semisweet chocolate baking bar

1. Line bottom and sides of a 9-inch square pan with aluminum foil, allowing 2 to 3 inches to extend over sides.

2. Combine first 6 ingredients in a heavy 2-qt. saucepan; cook over low heat, stirring constantly, until butter melts and mixture begins to thicken.

3. Remove from heat; stir in vanilla wafer crumbs, almonds, and coconut. Press evenly into pan; cover and chill 1 hour.

4. Spread Cream Filling over mixture in pan; cover and chill 1 hour. Lift from pan using foil as handles; cut into 1½ inch-squares. Place about ½-inch apart on a parchment paper-lined baking sheet.

5. Place chocolate in a zip-top plastic freezer bag; seal bag. Submerge in hot water until chocolate melts. Snip a tiny hole in bottom corner of bag with scissors; drizzle over bars. Chill 15 minutes or until set.

Cream Filling

MAKES 2 CUPS
HANDS-ON 5 MIN. TOTAL 5 MIN.

- ⅓ cup butter, softened
- 3 cups powdered sugar
- 3 to 4 Tbsp. milk
- ½ tsp. vanilla extract

Beat butter with an electric mixer at medium speed until creamy; gradually add powdered sugar alternately with milk, 1 Tbsp. at a time, until creamy. Beat in vanilla.

Yule Street Truffles *(1990)*

MAKES 3 DOZEN
HANDS-ON 15 MIN. TOTAL 45 MIN.

- 1 cup semisweet chocolate morsels
- 2 Tbsp. butter
- 1 Tbsp. brandy
- 1⅓ cups almonds, toasted and chopped
- ¼ cup powdered sugar
- ½ cup flaked coconut
- ½ cup whole pitted dates, chopped
- ¼ cup chopped red candied cherries

Microwave chocolate morsels and butter in a microwave-safe bowl at HIGH 1 to 1½ minutes, stirring every 30 seconds, until melted. Stir in brandy. Stir in ⅓ cup of the almonds and remaining ingredients. Shape mixture into ¾-inch balls, and roll in remaining almonds. Chill 30 minutes or until firm. Store in an airtight container in refrigerator.

Chocolate Peanut Butter Drops *(1992)*

MAKES 4 DOZEN
HANDS-ON 15 MIN. TOTAL 35 MIN.

- 1 cup sugar
- ½ cup light corn syrup
- ¼ cup honey
- 1⅓ cups crunchy peanut butter
- 4 cups chocolate-flavored frosted corn puff cereal
- Parchment paper

Combine first 3 ingredients in a 4-qt. saucepan; bring to a boil over medium heat, stirring constantly. Remove from heat; stir in peanut butter. Stir in cereal; drop by tablespoonfuls onto parchment paper-lined baking sheets. Cool completely (about 20 minutes).

White Chocolate Salties *(1992)*

MAKES 1½ POUNDS
HANDS-ON 15 MIN. TOTAL 35 MIN.

1   lb. vanilla-flavored candy coating, chopped
3   cups thin pretzel sticks
6   oz. cocktail peanuts
Parchment paper

Microwave candy coating in a microwave-safe bowl at MEDIUM 3 minutes, stirring every 30 seconds, or until melted. Stir in pretzels and peanuts. Drop by tablespoonfuls onto parchment paper-lined baking sheets. Chill 20 minutes or until firm.

Strawberry Fudge Balls *(1993)*

MAKES 4 DOZEN
HANDS-ON 20 MIN.
TOTAL 1 HR., 20 MIN.

1   cup semisweet chocolate morsels
1   (8-oz.) package cream cheese, softened
24 vanilla wafers, crushed (¾ cup)
¼   cup strawberry preserves
¾   cup finely chopped dried strawberries

1. Melt chocolate morsels in a small microwave-safe bowl at HIGH 1 minute or until melted, stirring after 30 seconds. Cool 5 minutes.

2. Beat cream cheese at medium speed with an electric mixer until smooth. Gradually add melted chocolate, beating until combined. Stir in vanilla wafer crumbs and strawberry preserves; cover and chill 1 hour.

3. Shape mixture into 1-inch balls; roll in dried strawberries. Store in an airtight container in refrigerator.

Turtle Candies *(1993)*

MAKES 16 CANDIES
HANDS-ON 20 MIN.
TOTAL 1 HR., 10 MIN.

1   (12-oz.) package semisweet chocolate morsels
Parchment paper
1¼ cups pecan halves, toasted
28 caramels, unwrapped
2   Tbsp. whipping cream

1. Microwave chocolate morsels in a microwave-safe bowl at HIGH 1 to 1½ minutes, stirring every 30 seconds, until melted. Cool 10 minutes, stirring occasionally, until slightly thickened.

2. Drop chocolate by tablespoonfuls onto a parchment paper-lined baking sheet, shaping into 16 (1½-inch) circles. Reserve remaining chocolate. Arrange 4 pecans over each circle; chill 15 minutes or until firm.

3. Microwave caramels and whipping cream in a medium microwave-safe bowl at HIGH 2 minutes or until caramels melt, stirring after 1 minute. Let stand 5 minutes or until slightly thickened. Spoon caramel mixture evenly over pecans.

4. Microwave remaining chocolate at HIGH 1 minute, stirring after 30 seconds; quickly spread chocolate over caramel mixture. Refrigerate 30 minutes or until firm.

Bittersweet Truffles *(1994)*

MAKES 3 DOZEN
HANDS-ON 15 MIN.
TOTAL 3 HR., 15 MIN.

½   cup butter
¾   cup unsweetened cocoa
1   (14-oz.) can sweetened condensed milk
1   tsp. vanilla extract
Unsweetened cocoa

1. Melt butter in a heavy 2-qt. saucepan over medium heat; stir in ¾ cup cocoa. Gradually add condensed milk, stirring constantly, until smooth. Cook over medium heat 3 minutes, stirring constantly, until thickened and smooth. Remove from heat; stir in vanilla. Pour mixture into a lightly greased 8-inch square pan; cover and chill 3 hours or until firm.

2. Use a small scoop to shape mixture into 1¼-inch balls; roll in additional cocoa. Store in an airtight container in refrigerator.

Orange-Pecan Truffles *(1994)*

MAKES 3 DOZEN
HANDS-ON 20 MIN.
TOTAL 2 HR., 20 MIN.

8   oz. semisweet chocolate baking bar, chopped
⅓   cup butter
1¼ cups finely chopped toasted pecans
¼   cup orange marmalade
2   Tbsp. orange liqueur
½   tsp. orange zest

1. Microwave chocolate and butter in a medium microwave-safe bowl at HIGH 1 minute or until melted, stirring after 30 seconds. Stir in ½ cup of the pecans, marmalade, liqueur, and zest. Cover and chill 2 hours or until firm.

2. Use a small scoop to shape mixture into ¾-inch balls; roll in remaining ¾ cup pecans. Store candy in airtight containers in refrigerator up to 3 weeks or freeze up to 12 months. Serve cold.

NOTE: You can substitute 2 tablespoons orange juice for liqueur.

Caramel O's *(1999)*

MAKES 3 DOZEN
HANDS-ON 15 MIN. TOTAL 45 MIN.

1	(14-oz.) package caramel candies, unwrapped
3	Tbsp. evaporated milk
1	cup chopped toasted pecans
4	cups sweetened 3-grain apple-and-cinnamon cereal

Microwave caramels and milk in a microwave-safe bowl according to package directions. Stir in pecans and cereal. Drop mixture by rounded tablespoonfuls onto a parchment paper-lined baking sheet. Chill 30 minutes or until firm.

Coffee Buttons *(1999)*

MAKES 2½ DOZEN
HANDS-ON 30 MIN.
TOTAL 1 HR., 30 MIN.

2	Tbsp. instant coffee granules
½	cup butter, softened
3	cups powdered sugar
2	Tbsp. coffee liqueur

Powdered sugar
Parchment paper

| 16 | oz. vanilla candy coating, chopped |
| 4 | oz. chocolate candy coating, chopped |

1. Crush instant coffee granules with back of a spoon or with a mortar and pestle to make coffee powder.

2. Beat butter at medium speed with an electric mixer until creamy; gradually add 1½ cups of the powdered sugar, beating until smooth. Add 2 Tbsp. liqueur and coffee powder; beat until blended. Add remaining 1½ cups powdered sugar, beating at low speed until blended. Shape mixture into 1-inch balls; roll in powdered sugar. Place on a parchment paper-lined baking sheet. Flatten to ¼-inch thickness; freeze 30 minutes or until firm.

3. Microwave vanilla candy coating in a medium microwave-safe bowl according to package directions. Place coffee rounds on tines of a fork; dip rounds in coating, letting excess drip. Return to baking sheet, and let stand 20 minutes or until set.

4. Place chocolate coating in a zip-top plastic freezer bag; seal bag. Submerge in hot water until chocolate melts. Snip a tiny hole in 1 corner of bag; drizzle chocolate over rounds. Let stand 10 minutes or until set. Store in an airtight container.

2000S

Buckeye Balls *(2000)*

MAKES 7 DOZEN
HANDS-ON 45 MIN.
TOTAL 1 HR., 15 MIN.

1	(16-oz.) jar creamy peanut butter
1	cup butter, softened
6½	cups powdered sugar

Parchment paper

| 1 | (12-oz.) package semisweet chocolate morsels |
| 2 | Tbsp. shortening |

1. Beat peanut butter and butter at medium speed with an electric mixer until blended. Gradually add powdered sugar, beating until blended. Shape into 1-inch balls; place on parchment paper-lined baking sheets. Chill 20 minutes or until firm.

2. Microwave chocolate and shortening in a medium microwave-safe bowl at HIGH 1 to 1½ minutes or until melted, stirring every 30 seconds. Remove several balls from refrigerator at a time; dip each ball in chocolate mixture until partially coated, and place on parchment paper-lined baking sheets. Let stand 10 minutes or until set. Store in an airtight container.

Raspberry Fudge Truffles *(2000)*

MAKES 6 DOZEN
HANDS-ON 40 MIN.
TOTAL 4 HR., 5 MIN.

1	(12-oz.) package semisweet chocolate morsels
2	(8-oz.) packages cream cheese, softened
1	cup seedless raspberry preserves
2	Tbsp. raspberry liqueur
45	vanilla wafers, finely crushed (1½ cups)
20	oz. chocolate candy coating, chopped

Parchment paper

| 3 | oz. red candy coating, chopped |
| 1 | Tbsp. shortening |

1. Microwave morsels in a medium microwave-safe bowl at HIGH 1 to 1½ minutes or until melted, stirring every 30 seconds. Let cool 5 minutes.

2. Beat cream cheese at medium speed with an electric mixer until smooth. Add melted chocolate, preserves, and liqueur, beating until blended. Stir in vanilla wafer crumbs; cover and chill 2 hours.

3. Shape mixture into 1-inch balls; cover and freeze 1 hour or until firm.

4. Microwave chocolate coating in a 4-cup glass measuring cup at MEDIUM 1½ to 2½ minutes or until melted, stirring every 30 seconds. Dip balls in coating; place on parchment paper-lined baking sheets. Let stand 15 minutes or until set.

5. Place red candy coating and shortening in a small zip-top plastic freezer bag; seal bag. Submerge in hot water until chocolate melts; knead until smooth. Snip a tiny hole in 1 corner of bag, and drizzle mixture over truffles. Let stand 10 minutes or until set. Store in an airtight container in refrigerator.

Texas Millionaires *(2000)*

MAKES 4 DOZEN
HANDS-ON 25 MIN.
TOTAL 1 HR., 45 MIN.

1	(14-oz.) package caramels, unwrapped
2	Tbsp. butter
3	cups toasted pecan halves
Parchment paper	
1	cup semisweet chocolate morsels
16	oz. vanilla candy coating, chopped

1. Cook caramels, butter, and 2 Tbsp. water in a heavy saucepan over low heat, stirring constantly, until melted and smooth. Stir in pecan halves. Cool in pan 5 minutes. Drop by tablespoonfuls onto parchment paper-lined baking sheets. Chill 1 hour or until firm.

2. Melt morsels and candy coating in a heavy saucepan over low heat, stirring until smooth. Dip caramel candies into chocolate mixture, allowing excess to drip off; place on parchment paper-lined baking sheets. Let stand 20 minutes or until firm.

Cola Candy *(2002)*

MAKES 2 DOZEN
HANDS-ON 15 MIN. TOTAL 50 MIN.,
INCLUDING COLA FROSTING

1	(11-oz.) box vanilla wafers, finely crushed (3 cups)
2	cups powdered sugar
1	cup chopped toasted pecans
½	cup cola soft drink
2	Tbsp. butter, melted
Cola Frosting	

Stir together first 5 ingredients; shape mixture into 1-inch balls. Cover and chill at least 30 minutes. Dip balls in Cola Frosting; chill until ready to serve.

Cola Frosting

MAKES 1 CUP
HANDS-ON 5 MIN. TOTAL 5 MIN.

¾	cup powdered sugar
¼	cup butter, softened
2	to 3 Tbsp. cola soft drink
¼	tsp. vanilla extract

Beat powdered sugar and butter at medium speed with an electric mixer until smooth. Beat in 2 Tbsp. cola and vanilla until blended, adding an additional 1 Tbsp. cola if needed to reach desired consistency.

Dark Chocolate Bonbons *(2002)*

MAKES 5 DOZEN
HANDS-ON 30 MIN. TOTAL 1 HR.,
15 MIN., INCLUDING VELVET FROSTING

6	oz. semisweet chocolate baking bar, chopped
5	Tbsp. unsalted butter
2	large eggs, lightly beaten
½	cup sugar
½	cup all-purpose flour
½	tsp. baking powder
1	tsp. vanilla extract
1	cup chopped almonds
Velvet Frosting	

1. Preheat oven to 375°F. Melt chocolate and butter in a heavy saucepan over low heat, stirring until smooth; remove from heat. Add eggs, stirring until blended. Stir in sugar and next 4 ingredients. Line miniature muffin pans with miniature baking cups; coat cups with cooking spray. Spoon chocolate mixture into cups, filling about half full.

2. Bake at 375°F for 8 minutes. Cool in pans 10 minutes. Spread Velvet Frosting over bonbons. Store in refrigerator. Serve chilled.

Velvet Frosting

MAKES 1 CUP
HANDS-ON 15 MIN. TOTAL 15 MIN.

½	cup whipping cream
¾	cup sugar
1	large egg yolk, lightly beaten
3	oz. unsweetened chocolate baking bar, chopped
2	Tbsp. butter, softened
2	tsp. vanilla extract

Bring whipping cream and sugar to a simmer in a heavy 2-qt. saucepan over medium heat, whisking constantly. Gradually whisk one-fourth of hot cream mixture into egg yolk; whisk yolk mixture into remaining cream mixture in saucepan. Cook over medium heat, whisking constantly, 6 minutes or until candy thermometer registers 160°F. Add chocolate and butter, stirring until smooth. Stir in vanilla.

Miniature Peanut Butter Cracker Bites
(2002)

**MAKES 3 DOZEN
HANDS-ON 15 MIN. TOTAL 30 MIN.**

6 oz. chocolate candy coating, chopped
1 Tbsp. shortening
3 dozen miniature round peanut butter-filled crackers
Parchment paper

1. Microwave candy coating and shortening in a small microwave-safe bowl at MEDIUM 1½ to 2 minutes, stirring every 30 seconds, or until melted.

2. Dip crackers in chocolate, and place on parchment paper-lined baking sheets. Chill 15 minutes or until coating is set.

After-the-Dance Pralines *(2003)*

**MAKES 20 PRALINES
HANDS-ON 10 MIN.
TOTAL 8 HR., 10 MIN.**

1 cup firmly packed light brown sugar
1 large egg white, beaten

1½ cups chopped pecans, lightly toasted
Parchment paper

Preheat oven to 400°F. Stir together brown sugar and beaten egg white, and fold in chopped pecans. Drop by heaping tablespoonfuls onto a parchment paper-lined baking sheet. Turn off oven; place baking sheet in oven, and let pralines stand 8 hours in oven.

Hazelnut-Chocolate Truffles *(2003)*

**MAKES 20 TRUFFLES
HANDS-ON 20 MIN.
TOTAL 2 HR., 20 MIN.**

1 cup finely chopped bittersweet chocolate
¾ cup whipping cream
2 Tbsp. hazelnut liqueur
1 Tbsp. unsalted butter
¾ cup hazelnuts, toasted
1 (3-oz.) dark chocolate bar, chopped

1. Place chocolate in a medium bowl. Bring cream to a simmer in a medium saucepan over medium-high heat; pour over chocolate, and let stand 1 minute. Whisk until smooth; whisk in hazelnut liqueur and butter. Place plastic wrap directly on surface of mixture; chill at least 2 hours or until firm.

2. Process hazelnuts in a food processor until ground. Place in a shallow dish. Shape chocolate mixture into 1-inch balls.

3. Microwave dark chocolate in a small microwave-safe bowl at HIGH 1 minute or until melted, stirring after 30 seconds. Roll each ball in 1 teaspoon of melted dark chocolate, and immediately roll in ground hazelnuts. Cover and chill truffles until ready to serve.

NOTE: For testing purposes, we used Ghirardelli Dark Chocolate for dark chocolate bar.

*Substitute ½ cup semisweet chocolate morsels for dark chocolate bar, if desired.

Rocky Road Peanut Butter Candy Cups *(2004)*

**MAKES 3 DOZEN
HANDS-ON 15 MIN.
TOTAL 1 HR., 15 MIN.**

1 (11-oz.) package peanut butter and milk chocolate morsels
2 Tbsp. creamy peanut butter
1 cup crisp rice cereal
1 cup miniature marshmallows
¾ cup chopped unsalted roasted peanuts

Microwave peanut butter and chocolate morsels in a large glass bowl at HIGH 1 to 1½ minutes or until melted, stirring every 30 seconds. Stir in 2 Tbsp. peanut butter until well blended. Stir in rice cereal, marshmallows, and chopped peanuts. Spoon mixture evenly into miniature paper candy cups. Chill 1 hour or until firm.

Hot-Spiced Bourbon Balls *(2007)*

**MAKES 2½ DOZEN
HANDS-ON 30 MIN.
TOTAL 1 HR., 30 MIN.**

1¼ cups powdered sugar
2 Tbsp. unsweetened cocoa
½ tsp. table salt
¼ tsp. ground cinnamon

¼ tsp. ground nutmeg

½ tsp. ground red pepper (optional)

¼ cup bourbon

2 Tbsp. sorghum*

1 cup coarsely chopped toasted pecans

60 vanilla wafers, finely crushed (about 2 cups)

Parchment paper

1. Sift together 1 cup of the powdered sugar, next 4 ingredients, and, if desired, ground red pepper. Stir together bourbon and sorghum. Gradually add powdered sugar mixture to bourbon mixture, stirring until blended. Stir in pecans and vanilla wafers; stir 1 minute. (Place a small amount of mixture in palm of hand, and make a fist around mixture, testing to be sure dough will hold its shape. If not, continue to stir in 20-second intervals.)

2. Shape mixture into 1-inch balls. Roll balls in remaining ¼ cup powdered sugar, and place on a parchment paper-lined baking sheet. Chill 1 hour or until slightly firm. Store in an airtight container in refrigerator up to 1 week.

*Molasses, honey, or cane syrup may be substituted.

Peanut Butter-Caramel Candy Bites with Colorful Candies *(2009)*

MAKES 2 DOZEN
HANDS-ON 20 MIN. TOTAL 40 MIN.

Preheat oven to 350°F. Shape 1 (16.5-oz.) package refrigerated peanut butter cookie dough into 24 (1-inch) balls, and place in cups of lightly greased miniature muffin pans. Bake 15 to 18 minutes or until edges are lightly browned. Remove from oven, and press 1 bite-size chocolate-covered caramel-peanut nougat bar into each cookie. Sprinkle cookies with 72 candy-coated chocolate pieces (3 pieces each).

NOTE: We tested with Snickers and M&Ms.

2010S

Triple-Chocolate Nut Clusters *(2010)*

MAKES 6 DOZEN
HANDS-ON 15 MIN.
TOTAL 4 HR., 15 MIN.

1 (16-oz.) jar dry-roasted peanuts

1 (9.75-oz.) can salted whole cashews

2 cups pecan pieces

36 oz. chocolate candy coating, coarsely chopped

1 (12-oz.) package semisweet chocolate morsels

1 (4-oz.) bittersweet chocolate baking bar, broken into pieces

1 Tbsp. shortening

1 tsp. vanilla extract

Parchment paper

Combine first 7 ingredients in a 5-qt. slow cooker; cover and cook on LOW 2 hours or until chocolate is melted. Stir in vanilla. Drop candy by heaping teaspoonfuls onto parchment paper-lined baking sheets. Let stand at least 2 hours or until firm. Store in an airtight container.

Bacon-Peanut Truffles *(2011)*

MAKES 2 DOZEN
HANDS-ON 30 MIN. TOTAL 4 HR.

¾ cup honey-roasted peanuts

2 Tbsp. dark brown sugar

¼ tsp. table salt

8 thick bacon slices, cooked

⅓ cup creamy peanut butter

Parchment paper

6 oz. bittersweet chocolate, chopped

1. Process first 3 ingredients and 6 of the bacon slices in a food processor 20 to 30 seconds or until finely ground. Stir together bacon mixture and peanut butter in a small bowl until smooth. Cover and chill 2 hours.

2. Shape rounded teaspoonfuls of bacon mixture into ¾-inch balls. Place on a parchment paper-lined baking sheet; chill 1 hour.

3. Chop remaining 2 bacon slices. Microwave chocolate in a microwave-safe bowl at HIGH 1 to 1½ minutes or until melted and smooth, stirring at 30 second intervals. Dip chilled bacon balls into chocolate. Place on a parchment paper-lined baking sheet. Immediately sprinkle tops with bacon. Chill 30 minutes before serving. Store in an airtight container in refrigerator up to 2 weeks.

Pound Cake Truffle Sampler *(2012)*

Million Dollar Pound Cake

MAKES 1 (9-INCH) LAYER
HANDS-ON 15 MIN.
TOTAL 2 HR., 30 MIN.

1   cup butter, softened
1½ cups sugar
3   large eggs
2   cups all-purpose soft-wheat flour
½   cup milk
½   tsp. almond extract
½   tsp. vanilla extract

1. Preheat oven to 300°F. Beat butter at medium speed with a heavy-duty electric stand mixer until creamy. Gradually add sugar, beating 3 to 5 minutes or until light and fluffy. Add eggs, 1 at a time, beating just until yellow disappears.

2. Add flour to butter mixture alternately with milk, beginning and ending with flour. Beat at low speed just until blended after each addition. Stir in extracts. Pour batter into a lightly greased and floured 9-inch round cake pan.

3. Bake at 300°F for 50 to 60 minutes or until a wooden pick inserted in center comes out clean. Cool in pan on a wire rack 10 minutes. Remove from pan to wire rack, and cool completely (about 1 hour).

NOTE: We tested with White Lily all-purpose wheat flour.

Vanilla Buttercream Frosting

MAKES 4½ CUPS
HANDS-ON 10 MIN. TOTAL 10 MIN.

1   cup butter, softened
¼   tsp. table salt
1   (32-oz.) package powdered sugar
6   to 7 Tbsp. milk
1   Tbsp. vanilla extract

Beat butter and salt at medium speed with an electric mixer 1 to 2 minutes or until creamy; gradually add powdered sugar alternately with 6 Tbsp. milk, beating at low speed until blended and smooth after each addition. Stir in vanilla. If desired, beat in remaining 1 Tbsp. milk, 1 tsp. at a time, until frosting reaches desired consistency.

Bourbon-Pecan Pound Cake Truffles

MAKES ABOUT 3 DOZEN

Crumble half of Million Dollar Pound Cake into a large bowl; stir in ½ cup Vanilla Buttercream Frosting, ⅓ cup chopped toasted pecans, and 2 Tbsp. bourbon until mixture holds its shape. Shape into 1-inch balls, and place on parchment paper. Roll truffles in ¾ cup finely chopped toasted pecans, and dust with powdered sugar.

Candied Ginger Pound Cake Truffles

MAKES ABOUT 3 DOZEN

1. Crumble half of Million Dollar Pound Cake into a large bowl; stir in ½ cup Vanilla Buttercream Frosting, ⅓ cup finely chopped crystallized ginger, and ¼ cup amaretto liqueur until mixture holds its shape. Shape into 1-inch balls, and place on parchment paper. Pour water to depth of 1 inch into bottom of a double boiler over medium heat. Bring to a boil; reduce heat, and simmer.

2. Place 2 (4-oz.) 60% cacao bittersweet chocolate baking bars, chopped, and 1 (4-oz.) semisweet chocolate baking bar, chopped, in top of double boiler over simmering water. Cook, stirring occasionally, 15 minutes or until melted. Remove from heat. Dip truffles in melted chocolate, and place on a parchment paper-lined baking sheet. Immediately sprinkle tops with finely chopped crystallized ginger.

Chocolate-Espresso Pound Cake Truffles

MAKES ABOUT 3 DOZEN

1. Crumble half of Million Dollar Pound Cake into a large bowl. Microwave 1 (4-oz.) semisweet chocolate baking bar and 3 Tbsp. heavy cream in a medium-size microwave-safe bowl at HIGH 1 to 1½ minutes or until melted and smooth, stirring at 30-second intervals.

2. Stir in 1 single-serve packet from a 0.93-oz. package of ready-brew Colombian medium-roast instant coffee (such as Starbucks Via). Stir ⅓ cup Vanilla Buttercream Frosting and chocolate mixture into crumbled cake until mixture holds its shape. Shape into 1-inch balls. Roll each truffle in Dutch process cocoa 2 times (this helps to get a good coating).

Raspberry Pound Cake Truffles

MAKES ABOUT 2½ DOZEN

1. Crumble half of Million Dollar Pound Cake into a large bowl; stir in ½ cup Vanilla Buttercream Frosting, ¼ cup seedless raspberry fruit spread, and ¼ tsp. vanilla extract until mixture holds its shape.

Shape into 1-inch balls, and place on parchment paper.

2. Roll truffles in ½ cup finely chopped toasted almonds, and top each with 2 toasted sliced almonds.

Chai Tea Truffles
(2013)

MAKES 4 DOZEN
HANDS-ON 15 MIN.
TOTAL 2 HR., 35 MIN.

¾ cup whipping cream
1½ tsp. ground cardamom
1 tsp. ground ginger
2 tsp. ground cinnamon
2¼ tsp. freshly ground black pepper
2 (12-oz.) packages semisweet chocolate morsels
⅔ cup Dutch-process unsweetened cocoa
½ cup powdered sugar
¼ tsp. kosher salt

1. Bring cream, 1 tsp. cardamom, ginger, ½ tsp. cinnamon, and ¼ tsp. pepper to a boil; remove from heat. Add semisweet chocolate morsels, and stir until melted. Pour into a lightly greased 11- x 7-inch baking dish. Chill 2 hours.

2. Remove from refrigerator, and let stand at room temperature for 20 minutes. Shape into 1-inch balls (about 2 tsp. per ball).

3. Whisk together cocoa, powdered sugar, remaining 2 tsp. pepper, remaining 1½ tsp. cinnamon, remaining ½ tsp. cardamom, and salt in a shallow dish, stirring with a whisk. Roll balls in cocoa mixture.

Coffee Chocolate Balls *(2014)*

MAKES 32 COOKIES
HANDS-ON 30 MIN. TOTAL 1 HR.

1 cup finely chopped almonds, toasted
60 vanilla wafers, finely crushed (about 2 cups)
½ cup powdered sugar
6 Tbsp. coffee liqueur
2 Tbsp. unsweetened cocoa
4½ tsp. light corn syrup
3 cups semisweet chocolate morsels
Parchment paper

1. Stir together first 6 ingredients until well blended. Shape mixture into 32 (1- to 1½-inch) balls.

2. Microwave morsels in a large microwave-safe bowl at HIGH 30 seconds; stir. Microwave 10 to 20 more seconds or until melted and smooth, stirring at 10-second intervals. Using a fork, toss balls in chocolate until thoroughly coated. Remove with fork; place on a parchment paper-lined jelly-roll pan. Chill 30 minutes or until chocolate is set. Refrigerate in an airtight container up to 1 week.

Coconut Snowballs *(2015)*

If the melted white chocolate is too firm after it is heated, stir in about ¼ teaspoon coconut oil.

MAKES ABOUT 2 DOZEN
HANDS-ON 10 MIN.
TOTAL 1 HR., 5 MIN.

½ cup unsalted butter, softened
½ cup powdered sugar
1 tsp. pure coconut extract or vanilla extract
1 cup all-purpose flour
½ cup unsweetened shredded coconut
Parchment paper
4 oz. white chocolate, chopped and melted according to package directions
Garnish: shaved coconut

1. Preheat oven to 400°F. Beat the butter and the sugar at medium speed with an electric mixer until creamy. Add the extract; beat 30 seconds. Gradually add the flour, beating at low speed until combined after each addition. Stir in the shredded coconut. (If the dough is soft, divide in half, and chill 30 minutes to 5 days.)

2. Drop the dough by level spoonfuls about 2 inches apart onto 2 parchment paper-lined baking sheets, using a 1-inch cookie scoop.

3. Bake, in batches, at 400°F for 7 to 9 minutes or until the cookies are golden brown on the bottom. Cool completely on a wire rack (about 30 minutes). Spread each cooled cookie with about ½ teaspoon melted chocolate.

Love it? GET IT

Entertain Section Opener (pages 8–9)

Copper pen: Paper Source, papersource.com; **stationery:** Crane & Co., crane.com; **stationery:** Paper Source, papersource.com; **cup and saucer:** Jasper Conran Wedgwood, wedgwood.com

Forest Feast (pages 10–29)

Wooden snowflake ornaments: Sage & Co., teters.com/sage; **birch sled:** Willow Group Ltd., willowgroupltd.com; **copper lantern:** Shiraleah, shiraleah.com; **hammered copper bowl:** Design Ideas, designideas.net; **crackle glass orb in centerpiece:** Sage & Co., teters.com/sage; **copper pod wreath:** Sage & Co., teters.com/sage; **mini birch baskets:** Willow Group, Ltd., willowgroupltd.com; **place mats:** Table Matters, table-matters.com; **chargers:** Vietri, vietri.com; **dinner plates:** Bambeco, bambeco.com; **salad plates:** Daniel Bellow Porcelain, danielbellow.com; **bark tree and containers:** Accent Decor, accentdecor.com; **amber glasses:** The Mayan Store, themayanstore.com; **trio of wooden wreaths:** Accent Decor, accentdecor.com; **pine cone candles:** Zodax, zodax.com; **appetizer plates:** Source and Tradition, sourceandtradition.com **bar cart:** HomArt, homart.com; **copper serving spoon:** Coal Creek Wood & Iron, rikkerswoodandiron.co; **earth glass serving bowl:** Vietri, vietri.com; **twig trivet:** Vance Kitira, vancekitira.com; **gravy boat:** Fat Cow Studios, fatcowstudios.com; **dessert plates:** Bambeco, bambeco.com

Hanging of the Green Brunch (pages 30–45)

Moss wreath: Davis Wholesale Florist, daviswholesaleflorist.com; **cement pots:** Leaf & Petal, leafnpetal.com; **bed swing and coverlet:** Pom Pom at Home, seibelsblog.blogspot.com; **throw and pillows:** Pottery Barn, potterybarn.com; **tray:** At Home Furnishings, athome-furnishings.com; **bar napkin:** Scents & Feel, scentsandfeel.com; **mercury glass pots:** Collier's Nursery, colliersnursery.com; **silver ornament wreath:** Accent Decor, accentdecor.com; **silver garland:** Creative Co-Op, creativecoop.com; **evergreen garland and wreath:** Gardens of the Blue Ridge, gardensoftheblueridge.com; **lemon cypress balls:** Mills Floral Company, millsfloral.com; **pear candles:** Vance Kitira, vancekitira.com; **flatware:** Pottery Barn, potterybarn.com; **gray dinner plates:** Costa Nova, costanova.com.pt; **plaid napkins:** Libeco Home Collection, libeco.com; **charcoal gray place mats:** Menu, store.menudesignshop.com; **white bowls:** Glenna from Anthropologie, anthropologie.com; **silver pears and pomegranates:** Saro Lifestyle, sarostore.com

Bake-and-Take Cookie Party (pages 46–61)

Galvanized and copper houses: Sage & Co., teters.com/sage; **tinsel and bead garland:** Sullivans, www.sullivangift.com; **mini**

copper cookware ornaments: Sur La Table, surlatable.com; **white glitter trees:** One Hundred 80°, At Home, athome.com; **galvanized tree ornaments:** HomArt, homart.com; **jingle bell sphere ornaments:** Shiraleah, shiraleah.com; **glass ornament garland:** Creative Co-Op, creativecoop.com; **enamelware canisters:** antique; **gold jingle bell wreath:** Shiraleah, shiraleah.com; **candy canes:** Hammond's Candies, hammondscandies.com; **galvanized and copper trays:** Roost, roostco.com; **evergreen tree wreath:** Collier's Nursery, colliersnursery.com

Starry Night Cocktail Party (pages 62–77)

Bamboo party picks: ACME Party Box Company, acmepartybox.com; **decorative trees and tree candles:** Zodax, zodax.com; **gold and marble cake stand:** ABC Carpet & Home, abchome.com; **white poinsettias:** Leaf & Petal, leafnpetal.com; **gold votive:** West Elm, westelm.com; **gold textured tray:** Roost, roostco.com; **wine bucket:** Shiraleah, shiraleah.com; **cocktail napkins:** Deborah Rhodes, deborahrhodes.com; **brass and glass star ornaments:** Shiraleah, shiraleah.com; **gold julep cups:** Davis Wholesale Florist, daviswholesaleflorist.com; **tree painting:** At Home, athome.com; **tall two-tone vases:** West Elm, westelm.com; **white light-up trees:** West Elm, westelm.com; **silver candles:** West Elm, westelm.com; **flowers, greenery, and filler:** Davis Wholesale Florist, daviswholesaleflorist.com; **boxwood garland:** Davis Wholesale Florist, daviswholesaleflorist.com; **cups and saucers:** Jasper Conran Wedgwood, wedgwood.com; **table linen:** Scents & Feel, scentsandfeel.com; **large metallic oval platter:** Be Home, be-home.com; **stemless champagne flutes:** Roost, roostco.com; **brass star votive:** At Home, athome.com; **faceted gold ornaments:** Shiraleah, shiraleah.com; **glitter ribbon:** May Arts Wholesale Ribbon Company, mayarts.com

Elegant Holiday Buffett (pages 78–95)

Wreath: grapevine spray-painted silver with painted grevillea tucked in; **Mercury glass candlesticks:** World Market, worldmarket.com; **textured Mercury glass votives:** West Elm, westelm.com; **smooth Mercury glass ornaments:** Pottery Barn, potterybarn.com; **julep cup candles:** Williams-Sonoma, williams-sonoma.com; **glass and silver vases (votives):** Davis Wholesale Florist, daviswholesaleflorist.com; **snowball tea lights:** Roost, roostco.com; **table linens:** Saro Lifestyle, sarostore.com; **appetizer plates:** Bromberg's, brombergs.com; **pewter trays:** Match, match1995.com; **orange carafe:** West Elm, westelm.com; **napkins:** Deborah Rhodes, deborahrhodes.com; **tall silver vases:** West Elm, westelm.com; **small orange dish:** MUD Australia, mudaustralia.com; **crystal cake stand:** Saro Lifestyle, sarostore.com

Thanks
TO THESE CONTRIBUTORS

Thanks to the following businesses

Anthropologie

At Home

Attic Antiques

Bromberg's

Chelsea Antique Mall

Collier's Nursery

Crate & Barrel

Crane & Co.

Davis Wholesale Florist

Fat Cow Studios

Gardens of Blue Ridge

Hall's Birmingham
Wholesale Florist

Hanna Antiques Mall

Henhouse Antiques

Hobby Lobby

Leaf & Petal

Lamb's Ears, Ltd.

Michaels

Oak Street Garden Shop

Paige Albright Orientals

Paper Source

Pottery Barn

Roost

Seibels

Shiraleah

Sur La Table

Table Matters

Tricia's Treasures

West Elm

Williams-Sonoma

World Market

Thanks to the following homeowners

The Hayslip Family

The Leak Family

The Reese Family

The Shallcross Family

The Wallace Family

General Index

Metric Equivalents

The recipes that appear in this cookbook use the standard United States method for measuring liquid and dry or solid ingredients (teaspoons, tablespoons, and cups). The information in the following charts is provided to help cooks outside the U.S. successfully use these recipes. All equivalents are approximate.

Metric Equivalents for Different Types of Ingredients

A standard cup measure of a dry or solid ingredient will vary in weight depending on the type of ingredient. A standard cup of liquid is the same volume for any type of liquid. Use the following chart when converting standard cup measures to grams (weight) or milliliters (volume).

Standard Cup	Fine Powder (ex. flour)	Grain (ex. rice)	Granular (ex. sugar)	Liquid Solids (ex. butter)	Liquid (ex. milk)
1	140 g	150 g	190 g	200 g	240 ml
¾	105 g	113 g	143 g	150 g	180 ml
⅔	93 g	100 g	125 g	133 g	160 ml
½	70 g	75 g	95 g	100 g	120 ml
⅓	47 g	50 g	63 g	67 g	80 ml
¼	35 g	38 g	48 g	50 g	60 ml
⅛	18 g	19 g	24 g	25 g	30 ml

Useful Equivalents for Liquid Ingredients by Volume

¼ tsp						=	1 ml	
½ tsp						=	2 ml	
1 tsp						=	5 ml	
3 tsp	=	1 Tbsp		=	½ fl oz	=	15 ml	
		2 Tbsp	=	⅛ cup	=	1 fl oz	=	30 ml
		4 Tbsp	=	¼ cup	=	2 fl oz	=	60 ml
		5⅓ Tbsp	=	⅓ cup	=	3 fl oz	=	80 ml
		8 Tbsp	=	½ cup	=	4 fl oz	=	120 ml
		10⅔ Tbsp	=	⅔ cup	=	5 fl oz	=	160 ml
		12 Tbsp	=	¾ cup	=	6 fl oz	=	180 ml
		16 Tbsp	=	1 cup	=	8 fl oz	=	240 ml
		1 pt	=	2 cups	=	16 fl oz	=	480 ml
		1 qt	=	4 cups	=	32 fl oz	=	960 ml
						33 fl oz	=	1000 ml = 1 l

Useful Equivalents for Dry Ingredients by Weight

(To convert ounces to grams, multiply the number of ounces by 30.)

1 oz	=	¹⁄₁₆ lb	=	30 g
4 oz	=	¼ lb	=	120 g
8 oz	=	½ lb	=	240 g
12 oz	=	¾ lb	=	360 g
16 oz	=	1 lb	=	480 g

Useful Equivalents for Length

(To convert inches to centimeters, multiply the number of inches by 2.5.)

1 in				=	2.5 cm		
6 in	=	½ ft		=	15 cm		
12 in	=	1 ft		=	30 cm		
36 in	=	3 ft	= 1 yd	=	90 cm		
40 in				=	100 cm	=	1 m

Useful Equivalents for Cooking/Oven Temperatures

	Fahrenheit	Celsius	Gas Mark
Freeze water	32° F	0° C	
Room temperature	68° F	20° C	
Boil water	212° F	100° C	
Bake	325° F	160° C	3
	350° F	180° C	4
	375° F	190° C	5
	400° F	200° C	6
	425° F	220° C	7
	450° F	230° C	8
Broil			Grill

Recipe Index

November 2016

SUNDAY	MONDAY	TUESDAY	WEDNESDAY
		1	2
6	7	8	9
13	14	15	16
20	21	22	23
27	28	29	30

THURSDAY	FRIDAY	SATURDAY
3	4	5
10	11	12
17	18	19
Thanksgiving 24	25	26

ULTIMATE HOLIDAY CHECKLIST

It is time to start planning to make this your best holiday ever!

EARLY TO MID-NOVEMBER

☐ Make a master gift list. Note homemade food gifts you're planning, and gratuities or gift cards too. Keep in mind teachers, babysitters, hairdresser, mailman, garbage collectors, etc.
☐ Stock up on stamps, wrapping paper, and supplies.
☐ Order holiday cards.

LATE NOVEMBER (AFTER THANKSGIVING)

☐ Shop Black Friday and Cyber Monday sales for discounts.
☐ Address holiday cards.
☐ Get decorations from storage.

EARLY DECEMBER

☐ Plan holiday menus. Place orders at any local shops or bakeries.
☐ Decorate! Trim the tree and hang wreaths, garlands.
☐ Finish shopping and wrap gifts.
☐ Mail holiday cards.

MID-DECEMBER

☐ Mail gifts to out-of-town recipients.
☐ Get guest rooms and baths ready for guests.
☐ Hit the grocery store for all nonperishable foods.
☐ Get cooking! Prepare make ahead dishes, and freeze them.

THE WEEK BEFORE CHRISTMAS

☐ Set the table, putting out all serving dishes and utensils you plan to use.
☐ Go to the grocery store for all fresh or perishable items.
☐ Finish any cooking that can be done in advance.
☐ Relax and enjoy your holiday!

December 2016

SUNDAY	MONDAY	TUESDAY	WEDNESDAY
4	5	6	7
11	12	13	14
18	19	20	21
Christmas 25	Boxing Day 26	27	28

THURSDAY	FRIDAY	SATURDAY
1	*2*	*3*
8	*9*	*10*
15	*16*	*17*
22	*23*	**Christmas Eve** *24*
29	*30*	*31*

CHOOSING A FRESH CHRISTMAS TREE

Follow these steps to finding your perfect match.

KNOW YOUR MAXIMUM SIZE

☐ Calculate your maximum tree size: Measure the height of your ceiling and subtract 1 foot. This allows ample room for your topper. Keep in mind that the smaller the room, the skinnier the tree should be.

CHECK FOR FRESHNESS ON THE LOT

☐ Run your fingers down a branch before you buy. All needles should remain intact, and your hand should smell like your evergreen of choice. Gentle shaking should also result in very little needle drop. Even with diligent care, cut trees only last about 10 days. Your best bet is to cut your own from a farm or to purchase one from a store or lot that offers trees harvested within days of delivery.

RECUT THE TRUNK ON AN ANGLE

☐ Once home, you're probably ready to decorate—but not before re-cutting the trunk about 1 inch above the butt end to aid in water absorption. If you don't have a saw, most tree lots will do this for you.

WATER FREQUENTLY

☐ Get your tree into a bucket of water within an hour of cutting, or the pores will seal with sap and your effort will be in vain. If the tree is fresh-cut from a farm, put it in the stand. Otherwise, soak it in a bucket of water outside overnight. You can also spray it down with a hose to remove debris and help hydrate the needles.

Decorating PLANNER

Here's a list of details and finishing touches you can use to tailor a picture-perfect house this holiday season.

Decorative materials needed

from the yard ....

from around the house ....

from the store ....

other ....

Holiday decorations

for the table ....

for the door ....

for the mantel ....

for the staircase ....

other ....

Holiday Meal-Preparation Tips

The secret to a successful meal begins with the right ingredients and equipment.
Take the time to plan your menu and organize your schedule to ensure great results.

PERFECT PLANNING

Your oven will get more use in the next two months than any other time of the year. Learn how to organize your menu and juggle recipes so everything comes out hot and on time.

Once you've decided on your menu, think through how to cook it. If all of your dishes have to go in the oven—and at different temperatures and times—you might have trouble. Modify your menu so that you get the turkey done first; then choreograph the rest of your prep time so that all your dishes come out together.

TURKEY TRICKS

It can take two to three days to thaw a frozen turkey in the refrigerator. So, buy it ahead of time while the selection is still good, and plan when and how you'll thaw it. Find defrosting charts attached to the turkey, or visit www.butterball.com.

After the turkey thaws, stick your hand into the cavity and pull out the neck and giblets. They're usually wrapped in paper. If you forget this step and find these after you've finished cooking, your turkey is still safe to eat; just pull 'em out, enjoy a laugh, and go on.

Once you remove the turkey from the oven, cover it loosely with foil to allow the bird to rest. The juices absorb back into the turkey, and it carves easily. This resting is prime oven time for additional casseroles or dessert.

GADGETS TO GET

☐ Bulb baster   ☐ Thermometer   ☐ Cheesecloth
☐ Turkey lifters   ☐ Roasting racks   ☐ Oven mitts
☐ Timer

GARLANDS, TREES & WREATHS OH MY!

We've been readying you for the holidays since 1966. In those 50 years, we've trimmed a forest of trees,
strung runways of garland, and hung countless wreaths. Through it all, we've tried and tested every idea imaginable.
We promise to have you and your home all ready soon so you can relax and enjoy the season. Our gift to you this year?
A high-style, low-fuss approach to wreaths, trees, and garlands and all the added touches that make the season special.

WREATHS

The only formula we follow for wreaths is to experiment. Embellish premade wreaths or fill do-it-yourself wreath forms with foraged evergreen clippings for festive options that can hang in just about any room in the house. Let nuts, berries, ornaments, and ribbons be the crowning jewels.

DOORWAY

With so much traffic, keep doors simple with a crisp swag over the top, accented with trailing ribbons and ornaments. To best secure the garland, hang it with nails placed right above the molding to minimize visible holes.

THE TREE

Take inspiration from the surrounding landscape to infuse your tree with festive spirit and local flavor—tuck in a profusion of palm fronds, oyster shell accents, and a beachy palette if yours is a seaside setting. Or tweak the look to suit your home's decor.

MANTEL

The fireplace is a holiday focal point. Adorn it accordingly with a single swag, letting the ends trail to the floor. Early in the season, accent with ribbons, dried botanicals, faux fruit, and silver brunia berries. When company's coming, update the look with fresh embellishments like cut flowers in florist water picks (secured with florist wire).

ORNAMENTS

The key to a perfectly imperfect-looking tree? A smartly curated mix of ornaments. We advise a five-type formula: three sizes of balls in shades that coordinate with your chosen palette, a star shape for edge, and a few one-of-a-kind ornaments for a collected, personal feel. Select ornaments in an array of reflective finishes to bounce light around the room and give the tree a layered, sparkly look.

STARRING ORNAMENTS

We all have cherished ornaments. These are the pieces that give our trees personality. They can be either fine collected objects or priceless handmade ones. Hang these from the tree with extra-long velvet ribbon so they will stand out from the others. If weighty, hang them 3 to 4 inches back from the tip of the branch to keep them secure.

GIFT TAGS

Rather than buying all your packaging supplies, forage for creative materials. Shop your yard for pinecones, leaves, pods, and acorns, and write on them with metallic paint pens. A slice of wood with bark attached makes a pretty tag for a simple brown paper package accented with an evergreen sprig from the tree.

TRIMMINGS

Every tree needs a garland that snakes its way from top to bottom and focuses attention on your ornament mix. From high-shine tinsel and more subtle ribbon woven through the branches to beads or strung fruit, options are abundant.

LIGHTS

As with the ornaments, choose lights in assorted shapes and sizes. We like the combo of classic white twinkle lights and larger round cafe lights to add brightness without having to wrap each branch. Start at the top, and wind down with one set. Then repeat with the second set.

CLIMBING THE STAIRS

Set an elegant tone with a cascade of boxwood and ribbon that attaches to the banister with coated wire and chenille stems to prevent scratching. For more formal events, dress up the garland with fresh flowers, succulents, and seeded eucalyptus in a florist foam cage attached to the newel post with trailing ribbon.

Party PLANNER

Stay on top of your party plans with our time-saving menu organizer.

GUESTS	WHAT THEY'RE BRINGING	SERVING PIECES NEEDED
....	☐ appetizer ☐ beverage ☐ bread ☐ main dish ☐ side dish ☐ dessert	....
....	☐ appetizer ☐ beverage ☐ bread ☐ main dish ☐ side dish ☐ dessert	....
....	☐ appetizer ☐ beverage ☐ bread ☐ main dish ☐ side dish ☐ dessert	....
....	☐ appetizer ☐ beverage ☐ bread ☐ main dish ☐ side dish ☐ dessert	....
....	☐ appetizer ☐ beverage ☐ bread ☐ main dish ☐ side dish ☐ dessert	....
....	☐ appetizer ☐ beverage ☐ bread ☐ main dish ☐ side dish ☐ dessert	....
....	☐ appetizer ☐ beverage ☐ bread ☐ main dish ☐ side dish ☐ dessert	....
....	☐ appetizer ☐ beverage ☐ bread ☐ main dish ☐ side dish ☐ dessert	....
....	☐ appetizer ☐ beverage ☐ bread ☐ main dish ☐ side dish ☐ dessert	....
....	☐ appetizer ☐ beverage ☐ bread ☐ main dish ☐ side dish ☐ dessert	....
....	☐ appetizer ☐ beverage ☐ bread ☐ main dish ☐ side dish ☐ dessert	....
....	☐ appetizer ☐ beverage ☐ bread ☐ main dish ☐ side dish ☐ dessert	....
....	☐ appetizer ☐ beverage ☐ bread ☐ main dish ☐ side dish ☐ dessert	....
....	☐ appetizer ☐ beverage ☐ bread ☐ main dish ☐ side dish ☐ dessert	....
....	☐ appetizer ☐ beverage ☐ bread ☐ main dish ☐ side dish ☐ dessert	....
....	☐ appetizer ☐ beverage ☐ bread ☐ main dish ☐ side dish ☐ dessert	....

PARTY GUEST LIST

....
....
....
....
....
....
....
....
....
....
....
....
....
....
....

GROCERY LIST

....
....
....
....
....
....
....
....
....
....
....
....
....

PARTY TO-DO LIST

....
....
....
....
....
....
....
....
....
....
....
....
....

Christmas Dinner PLANNER

Use this space to create a menu, to-do list, and guest list for your special holiday celebration.

MENU IDEAS

DINNER TO-DO LIST

CHRISTMAS DINNER GUEST LIST

Set a Stylish Table

Take inspiration from these festive table settings for every holiday meal, from a casual family breakfast to a glamorous fireside dinner.

FORMAL HOLIDAY LUNCH

Give a midday gathering the Midas touch with a table laden with golden accents. This luxe look elevates lunch to a must-attend event. Utilize wooden trays as chargers beneath gold china and gold-edged glass dessert plates. Vintage fabric pouches can hold place cards and do double duty as party favors for your guests.

ENCHANTING DINNER PARTY

Create a cozy woodland setting with birch log candleholders embellished with moss, twigs, and berries. Add faux-bois china and hints of gleaming gold to make the rustic tableau a little more refined, and scatter glass acorn ornaments across the table for added shine.

CHRISTMAS EVE CELEBRATION

Add drama to a classic holiday china pattern with an amped-up tablescape of red accents. Create a stunning focal point with red ribbons radiating from a centerpiece of roses and wrapped peppermint candies. Red chargers, napkins, stemware, and even red rental chairs will add modern flair and pop against a bright white tablecloth. Tape mini candy canes together to form petite easels for place cards.

FESTIVE CHRISTMAS BREAKFAST

For a laid-back family gathering, leave a pretty wooden table uncovered to keep the look unfussy. Use simple white china in interesting shapes, and rely on a mix of textures, like velvet, linen, and wood, for maximum impact. Make your own place cards with crafts store basics: Back a simple white name card with a second larger patterned card, thread a wide red velvet ribbon between the two on a plate, and your place settings will look like holiday gifts.

NEW YEAR'S EVE COCKTAIL SUPPER

Layer gold-rimmed china with mint green and pink for an unexpected but fresh holiday palette. Add a scattering of metallic confetti atop each place setting for a festive touch. Cut a slit in the tops of Champagne corks to serve as fun place card holders. For a final flourish, have a calligrapher pen the names of dinner guests on place cards.

Stock a Spirited Bar Cart

Stocking the ultimate drink cart means more than supplying it with libations. Here are some tips for having everything at your fingertips and more.

HAVE CHEESE STRAWS AT THE READY

These savory snacks freeze and thaw with ease, making them ideal small bites to stockpile.

INCLUDE FRESH FLOWERS

Vibrant red amaryllis contrast well with glass and metal bar carts. Arrange flowers in shakers or ice buckets for a clever touch.

LEAVE YOUR MARK

Wooden monogram stir sticks add a functional focal point and deviate from the standard monogram napkins you expect to see.

SKIP THE PAPER NAPKINS

Disposable napkins are cheaper up front, but you save in the long run with cotton. At Christmas, outfit your bar cart with tartan linens.

OPT FOR VINTAGE WARES

Handsome glasses instantly elevate a cart's look. Use mismatched finds for a more storied display than a straight-from-the-box set.

SERVE SOUTHERN STAPLES

Stay true to your roots with Southern-made essentials such as Elmer T. Lee bourbon (Kentucky), Corsair gin (Tennessee), and Jack Rudy tonic (South Carolina).

Gifts & Greetings

Keep up with family and friends' sizes, jot down gift ideas, and record purchases
in this convenient chart. Also, use it to keep track of addresses for your Christmas card list.

GIFT LIST AND SIZE CHARTS

NAME/SIZES	GIFT PURCHASED/MADE	SENT

name ....

jeans____ shirt____ sweater____ jacket____ shoes____ belt____

blouse____ skirt____ slacks____ dress____ suit____ coat____

pajamas____ robe____ hat____ gloves____ ring____

name ....

jeans____ shirt____ sweater____ jacket____ shoes____ belt____

blouse____ skirt____ slacks____ dress____ suit____ coat____

pajamas____ robe____ hat____ gloves____ ring____

name ....

jeans____ shirt____ sweater____ jacket____ shoes____ belt____

blouse____ skirt____ slacks____ dress____ suit____ coat____

pajamas____ robe____ hat____ gloves____ ring____

name ....

jeans____ shirt____ sweater____ jacket____ shoes____ belt____

blouse____ skirt____ slacks____ dress____ suit____ coat____

pajamas____ robe____ hat____ gloves____ ring____

name ....

jeans____ shirt____ sweater____ jacket____ shoes____ belt____

blouse____ skirt____ slacks____ dress____ suit____ coat____

pajamas____ robe____ hat____ gloves____ ring____

name ....

jeans____ shirt____ sweater____ jacket____ shoes____ belt____

blouse____ skirt____ slacks____ dress____ suit____ coat____

pajamas____ robe____ hat____ gloves____ ring____

name ....

jeans____ shirt____ sweater____ jacket____ shoes____ belt____

blouse____ skirt____ slacks____ dress____ suit____ coat____

pajamas____ robe____ hat____ gloves____ ring____